ICEMEN

ICEMEN

Mick Conefrey and Tim Jordan

B⬛XTREE

First published 1998 by Boxtree

This paperback edition published 1999 by Boxtree
an imprint of Macmillan Publishers Ltd
25 Eccleston Place, London SW1W 9NF
Basingstoke and Oxford

Associated companies throughout the world

ISBN 0 7522 1341 5

9 8 7 6 5 4 3 2 1

A CIP catalogue entry for this book is available from the British Library.

Typeset by SX Composing DTP, Rayleigh, Essex
Printed and bound by Mackays of Chatham plc, Chatham, Kent

Icemen is the companion to the major BBC 2 series.

Dedication
To Patricia Jordan and Stella Bruzzi

CONTENTS

ACKNOWLEDGEMENTS

The BBC TV series which this book accompanies was filmed in Canada, Greenland, Norway, Sweden, Russia, Italy, the United States, and Great Britain. The production team included Jim Dobel, Clare McGann, Satpal Nehal and Catherine Walker. The cameramen were Richard Ganniclift and Doug Hartington. The sound was recorded by Fraser Barber and Tony Burke, and the programmes edited by John MacAvoy and Charlie Monochrome. Our thanks are due to Clare Paterson, our executive producer at BBC Documentaries, for her advice and support, and to Charlie Carman, our editor at Boxtree.

For both the television series and the book we are grateful for the help provided by many organisations and individuals: Philippa Hogg, William Mills, and Shirley Sawtell at the Scott Polar Research Institute; Russ Gibbons and Sheldon Shackleford Randolph Cook of the Frederick Cook Society; Derek Fordham of the British Arctic Club; Dr Raimund Goerler of the Ohio State University; Susan Barr of the Norwegian Polar Institute; Kare Berg of the Fram Museum; Colonel Anzelotti of the Italian Air Force Museum; Colonel Fortuna of the Italian Air Ministry; Sven Lundstrom and Hakan Jorikson of the Andree Museum in Granna, Sweden; Fred Maclaren of the Explorers' Club of New York; Sergei Priamykov, Dr Grishchenko, Dr Loshchilov and Professor Bushuev at the Arctic and Antarctic Research Institute in St Petersburg; Dr Phil Cronenwett of Dartmouth College, New Hampshire; Genevieve LeMoine at the Peary-MacMillan Arctic Museum at Bowdoin College, Maine; The National Museum of Aviation, Bodo, Norway; The Lincoln Laboratory at the Massachusetts Institute of Technology; Kevin McMahon; David Scrivener; Audrey Balchen; Colonel Andrew Croft; Ernest Schofield; Alfred Stephenson; Sir Alexander Glen; Lady Butler of Saffron Walden; Edward Peary Stafford; Bert Stafford; Gertrude and Maria Nobile; Bette Hutchinson; Robert Bryce; Chauncey Loomis; Wayne Tobiasson; Herb Ueda; Kenn Harper; Will Steger; Dr Allen Counter; Dr Herbert Weiss; Robert Bates; Beekman Pool; Dr Oran Young; Admiral James D Watkins

U.S.N.; Admiral James Calvert U.S.N.; Vice-Admiral William Cowhill U.S.N.; Admiral Vladimir Chernavin; Commander Victor Alexeev; Nancy Fogelson; Pierre Berton; Tor Bomann–Larsen; Atle Gresli; Leif Andreasson; Toralv Lund; Jon Ulvensoen; Ulf Larsstuvold; Francis Spufford; Wally Herbert; Alan Marcus; Eckart Dege; Jack Hicks; Hank Levasseur; Per Lindstrand; George Echalook; Jayco Simonie; John Amagoalik; Minnie Allakariallak; Robert Hissu Peary; Dr Michael Stroud; Mats Forsberg; Yelena Smolina; Sheila MacDonald; Birger Amundsen; Michael Dolan and Gaynor Scattergood.

PICTURE ACKNOWLEDGEMENTS
Our thanks to the following for pictures in the book:
Andreemuseet p. 7 (top) and p. 8; Mick Conefrey pp. 14 and 15; Italian Air Force Museum, p. 10; Italian Air Ministry, p. 9 (top) and page 11; Library of Congress: pp. 1 and 2, p. 3 (bottom), p. 4 (top), p. 5 (bottom); National Archives: p. 4 (bottom), p. 5 (top), p. 6; The Ohio State University: p. 3 (top); Alfred Stephenson: p. 13. The photograph on page 12 is from J M Scott's *Gino Watkins* (Hodder and Stoughton/ London 1935).

Whilst every effort has been made to trace copyright holders for photos featured in this book, we would like to apologise should there have been any errors or omissions.

INTRODUCTION

There is no land whatsoever at the North Pole. Down south, the Antarctic is a continent surrounded by the sea, the South Pole a fixed point marked by a flag-pole. But with the Arctic, it is different.

At 66° 33' N you cross the imaginary line of the Arctic Circle. This means that there will be at least one period in the year of permanent daytime and one of permanent darkness. At about 70° you cross the tree-line, the real point after which there are no more trees. From now on most of the land is permafrost; though the top layer of soil may melt in summer, there can be up to a kilometre of permanently frozen ground beneath it. If you're coming from the North American side, at 83° N you leave Ward Hunt Island, the most northerly point of land, and walk out on to the frozen seas of the Arctic Ocean. From now on all you see is ice and water.

At 12.00 local time your shadow will point due north. Your compass, however, will not be so predictable. There are at least three Poles in the Arctic. The Pole of Relative Inaccessibility is the most obscure and least sought after. It is the furthermost point from land in all directions and is located at 83° 50' N and 160° W. The North Magnetic Pole – the point to which compass needles are trained – lies at latitude 78° 18' N. It was discovered in 1831 by the British explorer James Clark Ross, though subsequent explorers found that in fact it is continually moving due to fluctuations in the earth's magnetic field. The Geographic North Pole is located at latitude 90° N. This is the point where all directions are south, a mathematical concept grafted on to an intangible location. You cannot find your way there by compass alone. There are no geographical features, and the ice is almost certainly moving under your feet. The only point of reference is the sun. To know where you are, you have to measure its angle above the horizon with a sextant: at noon, using a set of tables, you can determine your latitude. With a reliable chronometer or timepiece, you can also discover your longitude, and fix your position. In modern times, you can simply read your co-ordinates from the dial of a global positioning system (GPS) handset.

At first it is hard going. You pass through the 'crush zone', where the floating pack ice grinds against the static coastal ice, creating ridges of frozen rubble up to fifty feet high, and temporary channels of open water known as 'leads'. Just beyond the crush zone there is often a broad channel, sometimes a mile wide; the first men to encounter it called it the Big Lead. If the temperature is low enough, a film of ice may form on its surface and allow you to cross. It may bend and sag under your weight, because frozen seawater is flexible.

The ice-pack of the Arctic Ocean is made up of thousands of individual 'ice-floes' which are in constant motion, driven by ocean currents and polar winds. Sometimes they come together to create hummocks and pressure ridges; sometimes they draw apart creating river-like leads and Arctic lakes or 'polynyas'. As you get closer to the Pole the ice becomes smoother and there are fewer pressure ridges or stretches of broken water.

For most of the year the Pole is covered in ice, though occasionally in the summer a polynya may drift over it, or the ice may be parted by a Russian ice-breaker or a visiting submarine. There is no reason to leave any markers for posterity; within three days a flag left at the North Pole may have drifted up to eighteen miles away. In spite of its elusiveness, for hundreds of years explorers have been drawn northwards, hoping to be able to say that they have reached the top of the world.

Before the outsiders came the Arctic had been inhabited for many thousands of years by the Inuit. They had no concept of the North Pole, didn't use compasses and couldn't quite see what all the fuss was about. They willingly worked for Europeans and unwillingly succumbed to all the 'civilised' diseases which they brought with them. Many of the early explorers were initially aghast at the idea of 'going native' but ultimately most realised that the Inuit attitude towards food, clothing and transport made good sense. All, however, to varying degrees, 'brought their environment' with them – in the words of explorer Vilhjalmur Stefansson. The British mounted heraldic pennants on their sledges which they man-hauled across the icy wilderness, the American Peary took 'readers' wives' nude pictures of his Inuit lover and when the airship *Italia* arrived at the Pole in 1928 its crew toasted each other with home-made advocaat as their wind-up gramophone cranked out the national anthem into the frozen air. For almost all the Icemen heroism was invariably matched by eccentricity, patriotism and personal ambition.

It is now a cliché that the race to the North Pole resembled the space race of the sixties, but the comparison remains valid. The Arctic shares the same flat barren lunar landscape; astronauts and explorers have both had to put up with extreme isolation, the moon and the Pole were both symbolic rather than real prizes. But there is also something else which shouldn't be forgotten: in 1909 the Peary/Cook controversy was front page news in Europe and America for three months. When Amundsen returned from his Arctic air expedition in 1925, the whole of Oslo came out to welcome him back. Today polar exploration rarely warrants more than a couple of column inches, but for much of this century the exploits of leading explorers were followed avidly all around the world.

Fortunately for us, most of the Icemen were relentless self-publicists and conscientious diarists. They had no choice. They wrote books to pay off the expeditions that they had just been on and to raise money to make their next dreams come true. Hubert Wilkins polished off his book *Under the North Pole* several months before he set off. Sometimes you can see the hand of the ghost writer, but many of the Icemen were surprisingly good authors. Andrée's polar diary, discovered thirty-three years after his lonely death on White Island, is an amazing document. Knud Rasmussen's ten-volume report on *The Fifth Thule Expedition* is a slightly more daunting proposition.

The first three chapters of *Icemen* look at the early history of Arctic exploration focusing on the search for the Northwest Passage and the race to the North Pole. The Peary/Cook controversy over who first reached the Pole is one of the most fascinating episodes in the history of exploration and still the subject of passionate debate. Then we move on to the Arctic fliers, going from Salomon Andrée's ill-fated balloon trip to Gino Watkins' British Arctic Air Route expedition of 1931. This was an era when machines became increasingly prominent, but nevertheless it produced some of the most eccentric characters and bizarre episodes in Arctic lore. In the final chapters we look at the post-war years when the Arctic ceased to be an arena for individual achievement but became increasingly important for geo-political reasons. Today we are all famil-iar with the history of the Cold War but few realise just how important the Arctic became in this period and the long-term effects it had on the people who live there.

We hugely enjoyed making the series and we hope that you enjoy this book. So wrap up warm, grab a husky, cradle a brandy, and read on . . .

Chapter One

THE MAN WHO ATE HIS SHOES

In the summer of 1845 two ships of a British naval expedition sailed into the uncharted labyrinth of Canada's Arctic islands, and vanished. By the time the British Admiralty struck the names of the 129 officers and men from its books nine years later, more than thirty relief expeditions had returned after finding no trace of the ships and no explanation for their disappearance. A mystery that enthralled the world seemed likely to have no solution until, a few months later, an officer of the Hudson's Bay Company had a chance encounter with some Eskimos in a remote part of the archipelago. Many of them wore ornaments of gold and silver. On these were crests and engravings from the long-missing expedition. Years before, members of their tribe had seen a party of white men; they had a story to tell him about their fate. In his letter to the Admiralty he warned that it was 'a fate as terrible as the imagination can conceive'.

The doomed ships of the Franklin expedition were searching for a northern sea route between the Atlantic and the Pacific. Its discovery was by now purely a matter of national prestige. But three hundred years earlier, when the British first went in search of the 'Northwest Passage', they had in mind a more tangible reward: a navigable trade route for merchant ships sailing to the Orient.

On the eastern edge of the Canadian archipelago, the bays and straits named after Frobisher, Davis, Baffin and Hudson memorialise the attempts of British mariners to sail over the top of the North American continent to the Spice Islands and Cathay. It was an age when a single cargo of cloves could make a merchant rich, and when the alternative routes, around the southern tips of Africa and America, were monopolised by the Spanish and Portuguese. In seeking a northern route, some were confused by fanciful maps drawn by the ancients, showing

Greenland joined to Europe and suggesting mid-Atlantic islands that never materialised. All proceeded with courage and optimism, not knowing that the geography of the Canadian Arctic was even more fantastic – in its complexity – than the charts on their tables. In 1576, when Martin Frobisher sailed into the bay named after him, he believed he was travelling between the continents of America and Asia. Further south, in 1610, Henry Hudson mistook an enormous bay for the Pacific Ocean; when the ice closed in the captain was cast adrift by a mutinous crew and never seen again. Both expeditions had sailed into dead ends on the eastern shores of the Canadian Arctic. The entrance to the inner archipelago, and therefore to the Northwest Passage, lay to the north in the great bay named after William Baffin. But Baffin mistook it for a dead end.

As early as the mid-seventeenth century, enough had been learnt to rule out the possibility of a commercial sea route to the Pacific, and interest in the Arctic subsided. If the Northwest Passage existed, it had to be far to the north, above the Arctic Circle, where heavy ice made navigation impossible for most – if not all – of the year. At these latitudes explorers' compasses behaved strangely, mirages appeared, ghostly fogs descended for weeks on end, while the pack ice cracked and groaned around their frail ships, threatening to envelop and crush them. Sudden storms swelled. In the winter the sun disappeared altogether, and with it, it seemed, all forms of life other than their own. It was a place of unredeemable desolation and obvious danger, from which commercially-minded explorers were happy to withdraw. There were more fruitful opportunities in other parts of the world.

Little was added to the maps before the nineteenth century. Two overland expeditions had reached the northern coast of the Canadian mainland, west of the Arctic archipelago. By sea, Captain James Cook had sought the Northwest Passage from the Pacific side, via the Bering Strait. He was greeted by an unbroken wall of ice more than twelve feet high drifting slowly towards him. Fearing that he would be pinned against the shore, he turned back at a place on the north-west coast of Alaska he named Icy Cape, and before Cook could return to try again he was murdered – in the more pleasant climate of Hawaii. Between Icy Cape and Baffin Bay the map of the Arctic showed a vast blank space marked 'parts unknown'.

At the conclusion of the Napoleonic Wars in 1815 there was only one challenge for which the all-conquering British Navy seemed ill-pre-pared: an era of peace. Though the vast majority of her 140,000 able seamen were discharged, most of the officers remained on the books, their careers in limbo. Many ships lay idle. The renewal of interest in the Arctic began by chance. William Scoresby, the leading whaling captain and Arctic expert of his day, who had sailed further north than anyone in history, reported a thaw in the sea ice around Greenland. Ice condi-tions were known to vary unpredictably from one year to the next, but nevertheless Scoresby was impressed by the extent of the thaw, and in a letter to the Royal Society suggested it was time for a resumption of Arctic exploration. His proposal was relayed to the Admiralty, where it reached the desk of the Second Secretary, John Barrow.

Barrow was immediately captivated by the idea of sending the Navy to complete the explorations Britain had begun three centuries before. Arguments were formulated in support of the proposal. If Britain did not claim the Arctic, then Russia or the United States might, enclosing the British territory of Canada; science had much to learn from the far north, and it was possible that this might lead to commercial benefits. Besides, naval voyages in these harsh climates would be an excellent test of men and equipment. In reality, it was the romance of the search that appealed to Barrow, and the national prestige that would come with the discovery of the passage. 'The Admiralty having done so much,' he wrote, 'it would be most mortifying and not very creditable to let another naval power complete what we had begun.'

It was an age of optimism and confidence in science. Barrow believed that not only was the passage obtainable, but the North Pole as well. In common with many geographers of the period, Barrow believed in the theory of an 'Open Polar Sea'. We know today that the North Pole lies in – or under – a permanently frozen ocean. Barrow thought other-wise. In 1818, when he read Scoresby's report, what lay above the 80th parallel was entirely unknown. Some believed in a polar vortex into which the oceans rushed: wasn't this the only explanation for the tides? Others preferred the ancient legend of Hyperborea ('the land beyond the north winds'), a temperate polar continent encircled by ice. The attrac-tive notion did not have much evidence to support it – just a little unexplained driftwood on the treeless coast of Greenland and northerly winds that were not always as icy as one might have expected. The Open Polar Sea, on to which a ship would sail if it could penetrate the encircling barrier of ice, was a more plausible theory, and one which was widely believed. Central to its logic was the observation that the further north one travels the longer are the 'days' of Arctic summer, during which the sun remains above the horizon. At the North Pole the constant summer sunlight would, it was thought, prevent the formation of sea ice during the season.

In 1818 two expeditions were dispatched by the British Navy. Captain David Buchan was ordered to sail due north through the strait between Greenland and Spitsbergen, find a way through the ice barrier on to the Open Polar Sea, and proceed to the North Pole. Captain John Ross's orders were to penetrate Davis Strait, between Greenland and Baffin Land, find a channel to the west, and sail through it in search of a passage to the Pacific. A measure of the British government's commitment to Arctic exploration is the Act of Parliament that set out a system of rewards: £20,000 waited for the first ship to find a northerly route to the Pacific. There were graduated rewards for penetrating the Arctic archipelago: £5,000 for the first ship to pass 110° W above the Arctic circle, £10,000 for 130°, and £15,000 for 150° W, on the mid-northern coast of Alaska.

Buchan's North Pole expedition ended west of Spitsbergen in a chastening storm, from which he retreated having failed on all counts. Ross was initially more successful. Having passed through Davis Strait, he met heavy ice in Baffin Bay, but was able to manoeuvre his two ships slowly northward along the west coast of Greenland.

Near Greenland's Cape York, in the north of Baffin Bay, an extraordinary encounter occurred. Several men suddenly appeared on the ice, hallooing and making 'strange gesticulations'. Ross's first thought was that they must be the survivors of a wrecked whaler, delirious with relief at the sight of a ship. In fact, they were a tribe of Eskimos who had never before seen white men or their ships. Apparently unable to decide whether to approach or flee from the strange apparition, the Eskimos hesitated some distance away. During the stand-off Ross ordered white flags to be hoisted. To lure the men forward gifts were deposited on the ice, and to express friendly intentions, a pole driven into a berg to which was attached a drawing of a sun, a moon, and a hand holding a sprig of heath. The expedition had brought an interpreter, and although their dialect was unfamiliar to him he was able to comprehend some of the words shouted across the ice: 'No, no – go away!'

Eventually the deadlock was broken by the gift of a knife. The Eskimos swarmed about the white men, intrigued by the strangeness of their appearance. What animal provided the skin for their clothes? Pointing to the ships they asked, 'What great creatures are those?' When they were told the ships were 'houses made of wood', they answered, 'No, they are alive, we have seen them move their wings.' An Eskimo approached the ship and looked up at the masts and sails, 'showing the greatest fear and astonishment'. Suddenly he shouted to it, 'Who are you? What are you? Where do you come from? Is it the sun or the moon?'

Ross followed the coast around the northern limit of Baffin Bay, passing the frozen entrances to Smith Sound and Jones Sound. The wider entrance to Lancaster Sound, however, was free of ice. This was the channel into the archipelago that William Baffin had judged to be a closed bay. Ross suspected he was right: there was no current emerging from it and the water carried no driftwood. Nevertheless he entered the channel and followed it westwards, through thick fog, the mast head and crow's-nest 'crowded with those who were most anxious'. After thirty miles, Ross saw, or thought he saw, 'a high ridge of mountains, extending directly across the bottom of the inlet'. The base of the ridge was obscured by fog, and Ross proceeded. For a short time the fog cleared, and Ross 'distinctly saw the land, round the bottom of the bay, forming a connected chain of mountains with those which extended along the north and south sides'. He named them the Croker Mountains, after the First Secretary of the Admiralty.

Nobody else seemed to have seen the mountains as clearly as Ross, and there was bitter disappointment among the officers when the order was given to turn back. Some of them simply did not believe the channel was a dead end. Had Ross seen a mirage? The phenomenon, known as a 'looming', is common in the Arctic. Soon after the ships reached London a controversy exploded. Neither expedition had achieved its objective. Buchan had failed because the objective was impossible, but Ross, it seemed to Barrow, had shown 'a want of perseverance'. He made his views public in a long critique of Ross's published narrative of the voyage. Having no doubt spoken to the officers of the expedition, Barrow was convinced that Lancaster Sound was the gateway to the passage, and that in turning back Ross had made a disastrous and unaccountable error of judgement. Ross strenuously defended his actions, but the naval establishment had made up its mind: he would not be given another command.

While Ross's career appeared to be in ruins, the two expeditions of 1818 led to the promotion – and eventual celebrity – of both men who were second-in-command. Barrow now planned two simultaneous expeditions to the Arctic, seeking the Northwest Passage from both the Atlantic and the western side. William Edward Parry, who had commanded Ross's secondary ship, was ordered to return to Lancaster Sound and sail westward through the illusory Croker Mountains. While he did so, a separate overland expedition would head for the mouth of the Coppermine River and move eastward by canoe along the coast of the Canadian mainland. Each expedition would be moving into a vast uncharted territory, at latitudes many hundreds of miles apart, yet Barrow – somewhat optimistically – seemed to believe the two parties could meet somewhere in the middle. Command of the overland party was given to John Franklin, Buchan's lieutenant on the failed North Pole expedition.

Franklin's career had led him into the thick of danger, and good fortune had brought him through more than once. He survived the worst of the battle of Copenhagen, saw most of those around him killed at Trafalgar, and escaped with a slight wound in the shoulder at New Orleans. Sent to Australia to survey the coastline, his ship (the *Porpoise*) struck a reef, leaving the crew marooned for fifty days on a sand bar just four feet above water level. Unassuming, even naïve, overweight and unfit, Franklin was not an inevitable choice to lead the gruelling expedition to the Coppermine's mouth. To reach it he would have to navigate wild rivers in brittle canoes and cross nearly 800 miles of territory that was largely unknown (except in the sense that it was known to contain hostile Indian tribes). But he was also tenacious, courageous and popular. The Canadian Indians were to call him 'the Great Chief who would not kill a mosquito'.

The two expeditions left England in 1819. When Parry reached the point in Lancaster Sound where the apparition of the Croker Mountains had appeared to Ross, 'breathless anxiety . . . was now visible on every countenance'. The men in the crow's-nest saw nothing but the continuation of the channel. Soon it was clear that the ships had sailed through the place on the map at which Ross had marked his mountains; their non-existence was proved. The crew celebrated. 'We were gazing on land that European eyes had never before beheld . . . and before us was the prospect of realising all our wishes, and of exalting the honour of our country.' Along the channel they passed islands, inlets and bays to north and south, giving them the names of prominent men. Attempting to head south into a broad inlet they named after the Prince Regent, they found their way blocked by heavy ice, retreated, and resumed their westward passage. The narrowing part of the channel they called Barrow Strait. On 4 September the ships passed 110° W, winning them £5,000 in prize money. The nearest point of land was named Bounty Cape.

Winter was approaching, the weather rapidly deteriorating. At Winter Harbour, on the southern shores of Melville Island, more than five hundred miles west of where Ross had seen the 'Croker Mountains', Parry prepared to spend the long Arctic night. It was to be the first endured by a British naval ship. The ice closed in, animals vanished, the sun set for the last time and 'deathlike' silence descended. Beneath the hatches the crew sang to the accompaniment of an organ and fortnightly theatricals were performed. Parry worked hard to keep them busy. None was allowed to wander far from his ship. When the dead of winter came temperatures fell until the thermometers cracked.

It was August of the next year, after nearly ten months of entrapment, before Parry was able to work his ships out of the ice. The channel to the west, however, was blocked by massive pack ice and further progress was impossible. Faced with the alternative of a second Arctic winter, with dwindling supplies and many of the crew already sick with scurvy, Parry decided to set a course for home.

Parry returned a hero. He had opened up 600 miles of the passage between the entrance to Lancaster Sound and his wintering station. Beyond Winter Harbour the channel was found to end in a colossal barrier of ice, but several inlets to the south had been charted. One of these, given favourable ice conditions, might prove to be the route through to the open seas of the west. Honours rained down on him: presentation at the court of King George IV, the freedom of his city, Bath, society invitations. Hundreds queued to tour his ship. His published account of the voyage, complete with illustrations, sold well, as did dozens of accounts of Arctic voyages in this period. The public discovered it had an appetite for tales from the weird and otherworldly landscapes of the Arctic.

Only one of Parry's ninety-four men did not return with him, but when

Franklin emerged from the Arctic after three years he had a very different story to tell. His small party, accompanied by Indian hunters and guides, and French-Canadian 'voyageurs' hired to man the canoes, reached the mouth of the Coppermine River in 1821, having spent the frozen winter in a hut they built at 'Fort Enterprise', north of the Great Slave Lake. In their frail canoes they travelled eastward some 500 miles on a broad channel of open water between the pack ice and the shore. No white man had seen this coast before. Franklin had hoped to come across an Eskimo settlement where the party could winter, but he found none. He gave the name of Point Turnagain to the easternmost limit of his journey. From here he decided to move overland in his retreat to Fort Enterprise rather than return to the Coppermine River. Supplies were by now dangerously low, and game scarce.

The journey to Fort Enterprise was a disaster. The hunters were unable to find game, the rugged terrain sapped their strength, and the party began to starve. Nine of the voyageurs died. One of the Indians resorted to cannibalising the bodies of the dead, then murdered the weakest of Franklin's officers; he was in turn shot and killed by the victim's comrades, as a matter of self-defence. Franklin was within a day or two of his own death by starvation when his advance party returned with Indian help. He and his companions had eaten hides, leather straps and their boots. Their 'ghastly countenances, dilated eyeballs, and sepulchral voices' horrified their rescuers. The Indians treated them with the 'utmost tenderness . . . and fed us as if we had been children; evincing humanity that would have done honour to the most civilised people'.

If Parry's stories of winter entrapment were captivating, Franklin's tale of starvation, cannibalism and murder was irresistible. 'The man who ate his shoes' became his epithet. In spite of the fact that the expedition ended in disaster – more than half the party of twenty had died – the British public found much to admire in Franklin's understated courage and stoicism. Nearly a century later they would find the same qualities in the story of Scott of the Antarctic. As far as the Northwest Passage was concerned, Franklin had achieved as much as Parry: 500 miles of the western part of the route between the Coppermine and Point Turnagain had been mapped and was proved to be navigable.

Using better equipment, a larger party and stronger boats, Franklin's second expedition of 1825–27 began with the navigation of the MacKenzie River to its outlet in the Polar Sea. From there they filled in most of the missing section of the map of the Canadian mainland's northern coast, between Icy Cape in the west, the limit of Captain Cook's incursion from the Pacific, and the mouth of the Coppermine River to the east. In his two overland expeditions Franklin had thus succeeded in mapping virtually the entire western half of the Northwest Passage.

On the eastern side, a route through the maze of frozen channels was proving more elusive, the ice more treacherous. Parry's second expedition probed the waters north of Hudson Bay, and found no way through. Returning to Lancaster Sound in command of his third expedition in 1824, Parry's *Fury* was driven aground in a gale under the forbidding cliffs of Somerset Island, then trapped by towering icebergs; her crew transferred to the *Hecla* and the expedition was aborted, having achieved nothing. However, the supplies of the stricken ship, taken ashore at Fury Beach, would be the salvation of the next expedition to Prince Regent Inlet. In the remainder of his Arctic career Parry never repeated the success of his first command. His expedition of 1827 in search of the North Pole was his last Arctic voyage. The reindeer he took with him to draw the heavy boat-sledges were no match for the rugged ice north of Spitsbergen, and were eventually eaten; an attempt to man-haul the sledges north, while the pack ice moved south under their feet, ended in exhaustion and failure.

John Ross had not forgotten his humiliation of 1818. The only way for him to live down the embarrassment of discovering a range of mountains that did not exist was to return to the Arctic and succeed spectacularly where he had failed before. The British Admiralty, whose First Secretary Ross had meant to honour in the naming of the Croker Mountains, would not give him an expedition, but Ross found an unlikely sponsor in a wealthy distiller whose name is still associated with gin: Felix Booth. For the first time, steam power would be employed against the ice. The paddle steamer *Victory* sailed from London in 1829; a contemporary painting shows her on the Thames, festooned with flags, pursued by a flotilla of small boats, hat-waving crowds gathered on the banks.

The ice of Prince Regent Inlet held the *Victory* for three consecutive winters. The Arctic landscape filled many explorers with awe, or even a sense of the sublime, but in his long entrapment Ross came simply to hate it:

*Amid all its brilliancy, this land, the land of ice and snow, has
ever been and ever will be a dull, dreary, heart-sinking,
monotonous waste, under the influence of which the very mind
is paralysed, ceasing to care or think.*

Prince Regent Inlet proved to be a dead end, but the expedition made
many important discoveries. The location of the Magnetic North Pole
was determined by James Clark Ross, nephew of the expedition leader,
on the Boothia Peninsula. He was so pleased that he declared 'nothing
now remained for us but to return home and be happy for the rest of our
days'. He took possession of the place in the name of the King. The
Eskimos who made their camps around the ship helped to supply the
expedition with fresh meat. This, Ross found, seemed to prevent the
onset of scurvy, which might otherwise have decimated his crew during
its long isolation:

> *all experience has shown that the use of oil and fat meats is the
> true secret of life in these frozen countries . . . many of the
> unhappy men who have perished from wintering in these
> climates, and whose histories are well known, might have been
> saved if they were aware of these facts, and had conformed, as
> is so generally prudent, to the usages and experience of the
> natives.*

Despite Ross's conclusions, the Admiralty held to the established view
on the prevention of scurvy: a little daily lime juice and 'active, cheerful
employment' worked as well as anything.

After three years of entrapment, Ross made the decision to abandon
the *Victory* and head north across the pack ice to Fury Beach and the
cache of provisions abandoned by Parry seven years before. From there,
using the boats abandoned by the *Fury*, they made for Barrow Strait –
only to find the channel choked with ice. The party retreated in despair
to Fury Beach, where their fourth winter was spent in a shelter made of
wood and canvas encased in walls of snow nine feet high. A Union Jack
was flown from the roof, and the house divided into officers' and seamen's quarters.

In August 1833 Ross and his twenty-two men – only one had died –
sailed their open boats into Baffin Bay and were rescued by the whaling

ship *Isabella*. It was a two-fold miracle: not only had Ross been given up for dead some two years before, but the *Isabella* was the very ship from which Ross had seen the 'Croker Mountains' on his first Arctic expedition.

Ross had successfully restored his reputation, though not as he had planned. By emerging from the wilderness after four winters, as if from the dead – and in such serendipitous circumstances – he won celebrity unprecedented for an Arctic explorer, and was knighted.

In 1845 Barrow mounted a 'final' expedition to close the gap between Lancaster Sound and the known lands to the south and west. He chose sister ships with a pedigree in ice navigation. Both the *Erebus* and *Terror* had made long voyages in Antarctic waters. The converted 'bomb vessels' of 370 tons had been designed to carry two three-ton mortars apiece, with speed sacrificed in favour of strength and stability. Their broad hulls accommodated the vast quantity of stores needed to sustain, in body and mind, a crew of some 130 for at least three years in the wilderness. Loaded aboard were thirty-five tons of flour, twenty-four tons of beef and pork, nearly two tons of tobacco, a ton of soap, two barrel-organs and a hundred bibles. The rigs were simplified, and in common with most ships bound for ice-infested waters, the bows of each were strengthened with additional timbers and iron sheathing. New technologies were used alongside old ones: a desalinator and a hot water central heating system were fitted, but more remarkable was the installation in the hold of a fifteen-ton railway locomotive to provide auxiliary steam power. Formerly of the London and Greenwich Railway Company, the engine was secured at right angles to the keel, a thirty-two-foot shaft connecting the driving wheel to an ingenious retractable propeller. The hand-picked crew were, in the words of a contemporary commentator, 'the elite of maritime England'.

Command of the expedition was given to Sir John Franklin. His courage and leadership qualities were unquestioned, but at fifty-nine he was considered by many, with good reason, to be too old for such work. However, the Admiralty could not agree on an alternative: Parry was fifty-four and retired; John Ross was now an old man; as for James Clark Ross, it had been a condition of his recent marriage that he stay on dry land. Franklin, the man 'who would not kill a mosquito', had recently returned from an uncomfortable period as governor of the penal colony of Van Diemen's Land (now Tasmania), where his liberal views and outspoken wife had earned him another epithet in the local newspapers: the 'man in petticoats'. So eager was Franklin to return to the Arctic and close his career gloriously with the first navigation of the Northwest Passage that his friend Parry told the first Lord of the Admiralty, 'If you don't let him go, the man will die of disappointment.'

On 19 May 1845, the *Erebus* and *Terror* sailed from London. 'I repeatedly waved my handkerchief – which I hope you saw,' wrote Franklin to his wife. A dove settling on the mast of the *Erebus* was considered a good omen. A monkey, given to the ship's officers by Lady Franklin, raised their spirits still higher. 'Never did an expedition sail under happier auspices,' reported *The Times*.

The sanguine mood was not shared by everyone in London. Sir John Ross expressed his concern at the lack of provision for any relief expedition – but Franklin dismissed his personal offer of a rescue mission as 'an absurdity'. The Arctic traveller Dr Richard King made plain his views that expeditions by ship were doomed to end in ice-entrapment; small overland parties would fare better. Bluntly, King warned the Admiralty that they were sending Franklin 'to form the nucleus of an iceberg'.

Franklin's orders stated that he should sail west along Lancaster Sound, past the opening of Prince Regent Inlet, and having reached Cape Walker, 'that every effort be used to endeavour to penetrate southward and westward' through the unknown sector of the archipelago. If this route proved impossible, he should try heading north from Lancaster Sound, past Cornwallis Island, in search of the 'Open Polar Sea'. In July cheerful letters were sent home from Greenland. James Fitzjames, second in command of the *Erebus*, told Barrow 'there is an incessant laugh from morning to night'. At the entrance to Lancaster Sound, on 26 July 1845, the two ships were sighted and approached by an Aberdeen whaling vessel, the *Enterprise*. The *Erebus* and *Terror* were never seen by white men again.

In London, news of the expedition's progress was not expected for at least a year. The ships would spend one winter in the archipelago and, if successful, would emerge in the Pacific the following autumn, news reaching London some months later. Time passed and nothing was heard. At the end of January 1847 Sir John Ross was the first to sound a note of alarm in a letter to the Admiralty. He urged them to consider the possibility that the ships were hopelessly entrapped, and to prepare relief expeditions without delay. The Lords of the Admiralty, however, decided to wait and see if the summer brought news. After all, the expedition carried supplies for fully three years.

By September the newspapers were expressing the national mood of growing anxiety, and the Admiralty were forced to concede that something had gone wrong. A reward of £20,000 was voted by Parliament to anyone giving assistance to Franklin and his men. Three relief expeditions were prepared for departure in 1848. Some measure of confidence remained, since the first relief ship was sent to wait for him to emerge in the west, north of the Bering Strait. A second party made its way down the MacKenzie River to search the mainland coast. The third expedition, commanded by James Clark Ross, whose wife had released him from his wedding pact on humanitarian grounds, retraced Franklin's route through Lancaster Sound to the heart of the archipelago. Franklin had been ordered to navigate the next southerly channel west of Prince Regent Inlet, if the ice permitted. But Peel Sound was found by one of James Clark Ross's sledging parties to be completely blocked.

While she waited again for news, Lady Franklin sought help outside the British establishment. She spoke to whaling captains in Shetland, secured from the Tsar of Russia an offer to search the Siberian coast, and urged President Taylor of the United States 'to take up the cause of humanity' and send an American expedition. In the meantime, she consulted a clairvoyant.

All three of the Admiralty's expeditions reported by November 1849 that they had found no trace of the *Erebus* and *Terror*. Ross returned the letter Lady Franklin had hoped would be given to her husband: 'My dearest love, may it be the will of God if you are not restored to us earlier that you should open this letter and that it may give you comfort in all your trials . . .'

Franklin had now been gone for more than four years. With the failure of the relief expeditions, anxiety reached fever pitch. To the newspaper-reading public it was a sensational mystery: how could two ships 'fitted and strengthened by every process of ingenuity, to meet and overcome every obstacle' simply vanish? What kind of a place is the Arctic, which can swallow up the 'elite of maritime England' without leaving a trace? Speculation about their fate and suggestions of where to direct the search covered the pages of newspapers and popular magazines. Franklin theorists gave public lectures, congregations prayed for those 'missing in the Arctic', and spiritual mediums sought guidance from the dead.

Public opinion demanded new and redoubled efforts to find Franklin. But in *The Times* a disillusioned voice spoke against 'any further waste of money and sacrifice of life . . . which, it is believed, will yield nothing but repeated disappointments'. Six men had died on Ross's relief expedition. Worse might follow. If new expeditions were sent, were they not likely to suffer the same fate as Franklin? John Barrow, the motivating force behind the search for the Northwest Passage, had died, and in some quarters it was felt that the British preoccupation with the Arctic should die with him.

For the time being it remained a minority view. In 1850 no fewer than six expeditions and twelve ships converged on the archipelago. They included an official Admiralty squadron of four ships, the first American searchers and a private expedition led by the 73-year-old Sir John Ross. Another was privately financed by Lady Franklin, for she was convinced they were searching in the wrong area. On the assumption that Franklin had failed to penetrate the ice of Peel Sound or any other southerly channel, they were looking to the north, since his secondary orders were to seek a northerly exit from the archipelago. Lady Franklin firmly believed that her husband had succeeded in making a way south, and ordered her ship to pursue this course. But like many ships before, Lady Franklin's *Prince Albert* was repelled by the ice.

As the *Prince Albert* returned in defeat to Baffin Bay, startling news was heard of a discovery at Beechey Island: the graves of three crewmen of the *Erebus* and *Terror* had been found, and the remains of a camp. The dates on the headstones told them Franklin had wintered at Beechey Island in 1845–6. At last a trace of the missing expedition had been found, but it did not help solve the puzzle. The area was scoured for any cached record that might have told the searchers where Franklin intended to go from Beechey, but none was found.

Not one of the six expeditions that departed in 1850 shed any further light on the mystery. The ships that remained in the Arctic for the winter experimented with – or perhaps just relieved the boredom by – firing rockets and flying kites, in the hope that any Franklin survivors would see their signals. More ingeniously, hydrogen-filled balloons were launched, carrying bundles of messages that were released at intervals by the burning of fuses of varying lengths. The messages were addressed in person 'To Sir John Franklin' and carried the co-ordinates of the rescue ships. The most optimistic strategy was the tagging of foxes, which presumably gambled on the four-footed messenger being shot for food by a survivor. It was the sort of tactic that paid off in boys' adventure stories, but in reality any hope of rescuing living survivors was fading away.

Every year new expeditions sailed north, and gradually most of the blanks on the map of the archipelago were filled in until only the northern extremities were unknown. The parliamentary prize for the discovery of the Northwest Passage was claimed by Robert McClure, although in scarcely glorious circumstances. He did not navigate from one side to the other, but walked for much of it. Approaching from the Bering Strait in the west, he was forced by a combination of the ice and his own recklessness to abandon his ship at the edge of the archipelago and proceed on foot through Viscount Melville Sound and Barrow Strait in order to be rescued by another search vessel. The feat of actually navigating a ship through the Northwest Passage was not accomplished until the next century.

It was 1854 when McClure returned to England and claimed his prize. The decision the same year by the Admiralty to remove the names of Franklin and his men from their books outraged Lady Franklin. With her husband's fate still unknown, such an action was 'presumptuous in the sight of God, as it will be felt to be indecorous, not to say indecent . . . in the eyes of men'. But her plea for a continuation of the search was doomed to failure by the sudden outbreak of war in the Crimea. Britain's ships were needed elsewhere.

Just when a line seemed to have been drawn under attempts to solve the mystery, *The Times* of 23 October 1854, announced: 'Evidence which may be fairly considered decisive has at last reached this country of the sad fate of Sir John Franklin and his brave companions.' It came from John Rae, an officer of the Hudson's Bay Company. While surveying the coast of Boothia Peninsula, south of Peel Sound, he had encountered a group of Eskimos. Four winters ago, they told him, members of their tribe had met a party of some thirty-five or forty white men, struggling southward on the ice towards the mainland. Using sign language the white men had explained their ship had been crushed by the ice, and they were going to where they expected to find deer to shoot. All looked thin. Later in the season, the Eskimos said, many bodies had been found to the south.

Some of the bodies had been buried; some were in a tent or tents; others under the boat, which had been turned over to form a shelter, and several lay scattered about in different directions . . . from the mutilated state of many of the corpses and the contents of the kettles, it is evident that our wretched countrymen had been driven to the last resort – cannibalism – as a means of prolonging existence.

Many relics were collected from the Eskimos: parts of guns, compasses, telescopes and watches that they had broken up to use as tools or ornaments. Among them was a silver plate engraved with Franklin's name.

'We do not trust ourselves to dwell,' wrote *The Times*, 'upon the horrors which obscured the dying hours of so many noble hearted men.' Many simply refused to believe it. Rae's report so far exceeded their worst fears that it must be untrue. Should the word of savages be trusted? Perhaps they murdered the weakened and starving men? In his weekly journal *Household Words*, Charles Dickens described the Eskimos as 'covetous, treacherous and cruel . . . a gross handful of uncivilised people, with a domesticity of blood and blubber'. In defence of Franklin's men, he argued that it was 'in the highest degree improbable that such men would, or could, in any extremity of hunger, alleviate the pains of starvation by this horrible means'. He cited several examples from the annals of exploration of British officers who, though dying of starvation, had not eaten each other. The gestures the Eskimos made to describe cannibalism (putting their teeth to their forearms) might have had some other meaning, he ventured, but what Dickens had in mind was unclear.

Replying, Rae defended the Eskimos, calling them 'decorous, obliging, unobtrusive, orderly, and friendly'. Generally honest, they made bad liars; he said: 'their fabrications are so silly and ridiculous, and it is so easy to make them contradict themselves by a slight cross-questioning, that the falsehood is easily discovered.' His respect for the Eskimos made Rae unpopular. From the accounts of his Arctic journeys, he appeared to live like them: he built snowhouses, drove dog sleds and depended on hunting for his food. In *Household Words* he felt it necessary to respond to the insinuation that his men enjoyed sexual relationships with the Eskimos. Rae categorically denied it, adding that this was more 'than most of the commanders of parties to the Arctic Sea can truthfully affirm'.

Rae demanded the £10,000 prize for resolving the Franklin mystery and eventually got it. He paid a courtesy visit to Lady Franklin, but she found him 'hairy and disagreeable'. She was not finished with the search – only thirty or forty men had been accounted for, and these only through the Eskimos' stories. No expedition had reached the site of the disaster. Furthermore, her conviction that her husband had followed his primary orders and forced a way south had been proved right by Rae's report. All along, the Admiralty had been looking in the wrong place. Now she intended to prove that, en route to his death, Franklin, not McClure, had discovered the Northwest Passage.

Lady Franklin purchased a small steam yacht, the *Fox*, and appointed Francis Leopold McClintock, who had served under James Clark Ross on his 1848 relief expedition, as commander. Departing in 1857, the *Fox* was held in the ice of Baffin Bay for the first winter, but reached Bellot Strait, a narrow, impassable channel between Prince Regent Inlet and Peel Sound, in time for the second. In April 1859 his sledging parties made contact with Rae's Eskimos, who confirmed the stories they had told him, and added that two ships had been seen west of King William Island, to the south of Peel Sound. One had been seen to sink; the other had been driven against the shore by the ice. Most of the wood the Eskimos possessed had been taken from it. They had lit fires to bring down the masts. Searching the ship for useful and decorative materials, they had found a single corpse of a large man with long teeth. Of the white men who had left the ship, an elderly Eskimo woman said 'they fell down and died as they walked along'.

McClintock dispatched his lieutenant, Robert Hobson, to explore the west coast of King William Island, while he moved southward along the eastern shore. Just after midnight on 24 May, McClintock found himself looking down at a human skeleton. It was lying on its face. The bones had been bleached white. Nearby was a clothes brush and pocket comb. McClintock pressed on. As he moved around the south of the island he found the cairn Hobson left to mark the limit of his journey down the western coast, and an astonishing message from his lieutenant. There had been no sign of the wrecked ship, but Hobson had discovered a cairn on the north-west coast, containing a written record left by the Franklin expedition. No other record was ever found. Though brief, it said enough to solve the mystery.

The document Hobson found was a standard Navy form, intended for message-bottles thrown from ships, bearing the formal request in six languages for the discoverer to forward it to the Secretary of the Admiralty. On it two messages had been hand-written. The first, dated 28 May 1847, stated that the *Erebus* and *Terror* had spent the first winter at Beechey Island, and after circumnavigating Cornwallis Island, had penetrated Peel Sound and beyond, to a point twelve miles north of King William Island. Here the second winter was spent, apparently without serious mishap: 'All well,' the message said. The second message, added in the margins nearly a year later, revealed the cause of the disaster: the ships had not been released from the ice since it closed around them in September 1846.

> April 25, 1848. H. M. ships 'Terror' and 'Erebus' were deserted
> on the 22nd April, 5 leagues NNW of this, having been beset
> since 12th September, 1846. The officers and crew, consisting of
> 105 souls . . . landed here . . . Sir John Franklin died on the 11th
> June, 1847; and the total loss by deaths in the expedition has
> been to this date 9 officers and 15 men.

A fateful postscript added that they intended to set off for what is now called the Back River, on the Canadian mainland, nearly 200 miles to their south. It was a desperate gamble to save their lives. 'A sad tale was never told in fewer words,' wrote McClintock.

Heading north along the west side of King William Island, McClintock found an enormous boat that the men had evidently tried to drag south, in the hope that it could be used on the Back River. Hobson too had seen it on his way north. Twenty-seven feet long and weighing 700 or 800 pounds, it was mounted on 'a sledge of unusual strength and weight'. McClintock estimated that it would take at least seven strong and healthy men to move it.

'There was that in the boat which transfixed us with awe. It was portions of two human skeletons.' One was wrapped in furs; the skulls of both were missing. If McClintock was transfixed by the skeletons that had been sitting in the boat for a decade, he was amazed by what surrounded them. There were silk handkerchiefs, towels, soap, tooth brushes and hair-combs, books (including *Christian Melodies* and *The Vicar of Wakefield*), cutlery, plates, 'in short, a quantity of articles of one description or another truly astonishing in variety, and such as, for the most part, modern sledge travellers in these regions would consider a mere accumulation of dead weight, but slightly useful, and very likely to break down the strength of the sledge-crews'. The boat told him everything he needed to know about the hopelessness of their attempt to reach the Back River.

McClintock returned to London in September 1859 with the final solution of the Franklin mystery, and was knighted for it. For Lady Franklin there was the news that she had been a widow for twelve years, and the consolation that her husband's expedition had, until the ice entrapped the ships for the last time, achieved more than any other in the quest for the Northwest Passage. McClintock was among those who argued that in reaching King William Island Franklin and his men had effectively 'forged the last link with their lives'.

The British era of large-scale expeditions that 'brought their environment with them' in ponderous warships, and used massive, man-hauled sledges, was at an end. In the future, the most successful Arctic explorers would be the ones who learned from the Eskimos and secured their help, travelling in small parties drawn by dog sledge, living off the land. The long search for Franklin had gradually unravelled the mysteries of the archipelago and produced a map; now only its northern limits were blank. Beyond these 'parts unknown' lay a new Grail of Arctic exploration. The North Pole was about to become the object of a twenty-year siege by an American explorer who would prove himself the antithesis of the man 'who would not kill a mosquito'.

Chapter Two

THE THING THAT I MUST DO

On the silent shore of Lady Franklin Bay, on the north-east coast of Ellesmere Island, preserved by their remoteness, three tiny wooden huts stand in the deep snow. Littered about them are the remnants of a Victorian expedition: barrel hoops, tin cans and, protruding strangely from the deep snow, several iron bedsteads. It is a ghostly place.

'Fort Conger' had been the northernmost base of the notorious Lady Franklin Bay Expedition of A. W. Greely. When Greely and his men left Conger in 1884 with two years of successful work behind them, they were doomed. Unaware that their supply ships had failed to reach the rendezvous point – one driven back by the sea ice, the next crushed and sunk – they were condemned to an Arctic winter without proper shelter or provisions. Eighteen of the party of twenty-five succumbed to the cold, to starvation and to scurvy. The survivors resorted to cannibalism. This much-publicised disaster cast a chill shadow over American exploration of the High Arctic in the last decades of the nineteenth century.

Fort Conger lay undisturbed for fifteen years. The next human to see it, and set foot in it, arrived during the long Arctic night, in January 1899. He had travelled for six days by dog sledge in fleeting moonlight, and latterly 'in complete darkness and over a chaos of broken and heaved-up ice'. His party was exhausted and low on supplies. They had begun eating their dogs. A dim light fashioned from a saucer, olive oil and a strip of towel revealed the quarters as Greely's men had left them: a disorder of packing cases, discarded furs, coffee containers, a few biscuits, papers. The new arrival ordered fires to be started in the iron stoves. There was 'a suspicious wooden feeling' in his feet.

Matt . . . inserted the blade of his knife under the top of Peary's

*sealskin boots. He ripped the boots from both feet, and gently
removed the rabbit-skin undershoes. Both legs were a bloodless
white up to the knee, and, as Matt ripped off the under-shoes,
several toes from each foot clung to the hide and snapped off at
the first joint.*

*'My God, Lieutenant! Why didn't you tell me your feet were
frozen?' Matt cried.*

His frostbitten feet were bathed in buckets of snow. With a hand knife, parts of eight toes were cut away. For six weeks Peary lay helpless, 'listening to the howling of the winter winds and the cries of my starving dogs', not knowing if he would avoid the amputation of his feet. Circumstances that to most would have spelt the end of the road were to Peary a setback. 'I *knew* that I should yet do the work which I had set before myself': to be the first man to stand on the top of the world. For twenty years he was driven by the conviction that he would reach the Pole, and reach it first, and that it would reward him with the immortality of fame. On the wall of the hut he pencilled a quotation from Seneca: '*Inveniam viam aut faciam*': I shall find a way or make one.

Robert Edwin Peary was a United States Navy Civil Engineer from the state of Maine. Tall, muscular, inexhaustible, fiercely single-minded, Peary deserved his reputation as a hard man. Yet he was also a mummy's boy. Mary Peary was widowed before her only child reached his third birthday, and devoted the rest of her life to 'Bertie'. A hypochondriac herself, she tended to over-protect her son, making him wear a bonnet to shield his fair complexion, ignoring his mischief, which included swearing in front of visiting clergymen and tripping up his grandfather. When he went to college twenty miles from home she moved to be with him. Sensitive about his living arrangements and his lisp, he was inclined to be solitary, making long walks through the coastal woodlands where he would collect specimens for his hobby of taxidermy.

Irked by a sense of social inferiority, he set himself courses of self-improvement and worked hard to make himself agreeable. 'I should like to gain that attractive personality that when I was with a person, they would always have to like me, whether they wanted to or not.' It was an ambition he never achieved.

Long before he took a serious interest in the Arctic, Peary knew he wanted to be famous. After two years in the offices of the United States Coast and Geodetic Survey, he thought his opportunity had arrived when he was recruited for the 'Inter-Oceanic Ship Canal' project, which at that time was surveying the jungles of Nicaragua (the canal would eventually be built in Panama). Thrilled by his adventures in the steaming jungles, he was unhappy back at his desk, and it was while 'prowling about' in a second-hand bookstore that he happened upon an account of Baron Nordenskjöld's *Exploration of Interior Greenland*. From this moment the Arctic had a grip on him that it never released.

As a child he had read Elisha Kent Kane's accounts of his Arctic explorations, but now Peary threw all his energy into learning everything he could about the history and practice of Arctic travel from the writings of Hayes, Hall, Nares and Greely. Within months he had formulated strong opinions: the British model of several ships and large parties was outdated; it was time for 'a new plan of a small party depending largely on native assistance'.

This was unconventional rather than original, for other explorers – notably Charles Francis Hall – had travelled with Eskimos. But the God-fearing Hall would have blushed at Peary's frankness on the subject of women in polar exploration:

> It is asking too much of masculine human nature to expect it to
> remain in an Arctic climate enduring constant hardship, without
> one relieving feature. Feminine companionship not only causes
> greater contentment, but as a matter of both mental and
> physical health and the retention of the top notch of manhood it
> is an absolute necessity.

He already had a plan for the attainment of the Pole: caches of supplies should be established along the route north between Ellesmere Island and Greenland, all the way to the shores of the Arctic Ocean. Here the party should bide its time until conditions on the pack ice were favourable. 'Such an expedition,' he concluded, 'can when the moment arrives shoot forward to the Pole like a ball from a cannon.'

Peary needed to make a start, and his attention focused on Greenland. In 1886 the interior and northern limits of Greenland were unknown. It had not yet been proved an island, and some thought the land might extend many hundred miles farther north, even to the Pole itself. The 'Great Inland Ice', devoid of life and land features, a place of hostile storms and treacherous crevasses, had scarcely been penetrated and never traversed. With $500 borrowed from his mother and six months' leave from the Navy he set off for Newfoundland to find a whaler that would take him north. It was Peary's intention to make a name for himself by travelling further and to a greater elevation on the Greenland ice than any man before him.

Three days were spent simply finding a way up the ice cliffs on to the outer rim of the cap. From there, progress over the white desert was a matter of determination, stamina and luck. Peary had been fortunate to find an enthusiastic Danish companion on the coast. Had he ventured alone across the hidden crevasses of the ice-cap edge he might easily have descended into permanent obscurity. As it was, they slipped at the jaws of crevasses, fell through the thin ice of glacial ponds, but were able to scramble to safety. Dazzling sunlight burned their eyes; in cloudy weather a 'white-out' erased all distinction between snow and sky until they were merely treading in white space. High winds from the interior brought vicious sleet and snow. They dragged their sledge for two weeks towards the centre of the cap, by which time they had travelled about 100 miles and reached an elevation of 7525 feet. Retreating before the wind, a sail and rudder rigged on his sledge, Peary was in high spirits. He had seen enough to confirm his conviction that this was 'the northern region which holds my future name'.

Although it was a modest expedition, made in the southerly latitudes of Greenland, it brought his name to the attention of scientific circles. Peary was convinced he had made a breakthrough. He told his mother:

> with the prestige of my summer's work, and the assistance of friends who I have made this winter, I will next winter be one of the foremost in the highest Circles in the capital, and make powerful friends with whom I can shape my future instead of letting it come as it will . . . remember, Mother, I must have fame . . .

His report in the Bulletin of the American Geographical Society was accompanied by a detailed proposal for an expedition to complete the first crossing of the Greenland ice cap. However, the Greely disaster had made support for any American Arctic expedition hard to come by.

Young, fearless, inexperienced, Peary was a risk that nobody wanted to take on. He was bitterly disappointed.

Returning to Nicaragua, the promise he had shown earlier was rewarded with his appointment as 'sub-chief engineer'. In charge of all the surveying work, and of some 150 men, he had little time to brood on his disappointment. A new route was mapped, and again Peary distinguished himself both as an engineer and as a leader of a complex expedition. He was innovative, brilliantly organised, and did not tolerate malingerers. Above all he relished being in charge.

In August 1888 he married Josephine Diebitsch, daughter of a professor at the Smithsonian Institution in Washington. They honeymooned in Seabright, New Jersey, with Peary's mother, and for a while he put aside the canal and the future, and devoted his time to Jo.

Six weeks later Peary read something that abruptly took the wind out of his sails: the Norwegian explorer Fridtjof Nansen had completed the first crossing of the Greenland ice cap. He had not forgotten about the Arctic, and now he watched with bitter envy as a rival enjoyed the credit for something he had wanted, and planned, and almost pleaded to do. Nansen, he felt, had stolen something from him. Peary resolved to upstage him.

Nansen had made his crossing in the south; now Peary proposed a more challenging traverse in higher latitudes, on a route that would take him into the unexplored north-east territory. Only two areas of the Arctic remained blank on the map: east of Ellesmere, and this part of Greenland and whatever lay to the north of it. What was known of Greenland had been mapped until that time by travelling along the coasts. Peary was proposing to 'explore Greenland from the inside' in order to determine its northern limit. Privately, he was wondering if it might prove to be an 'Imperial Highway' towards the Pole.

After nearly two years of lobbying and a series of lectures based on his summer expedition, Peary won the support of the American Geographical Society, the Brooklyn Institute and the Philadelphia Academy of Natural Sciences. The balance of the $10,000 budget was to come from nine independent scientists and private individuals in return for their passage to Greenland. The main party, which would spend the winter in the vicinity of Whale Sound before moving on to the ice in the early spring, numbered just seven.

Matthew Henson was Peary's black manservant from his second

Nicaraguan expedition. He had met him in a Washington hat shop. The storekeeper sold Peary a sun helmet, and on hearing he was looking for a 'boy' to take with him, recommended his young clerk. Henson had already led an extraordinary life. After running away to sea at the age of twelve he had travelled the globe, and during his many long voyages received a good education from a elderly sea captain who took him under his wing. Intelligent and adaptable, Henson had impressed Peary in Nicaragua. Now his 'bodyservant' was promised an unpaid adventure as sledge builder, dog-driver and jack-of-all-trades.

Frederick A. Cook, a New York physician, was 'surgeon and ethnologist'. The others were Langdon Gibson, 'orthnithologist and chief hunter'; Eivind Astrup, an experienced skier from Norway; John Verhoeff, nominally 'mineralogist and meteorologist', in reality a young sportsman who had contributed generously to the costs of the expedition; and, to the amazement of everyone and the consternation of some, Peary's wife, Jo. No white woman had ever wintered in the High Arctic.

The North Greenland Expedition left Brooklyn on 6 June 1891 on the *Kite*, and soon the 280-ton sealing ship was forcing and ramming her way through the ice of Baffin Bay. Peary had written to his mother of his confidence that he would be 'carried safely and successfully through', but even before they reached Whale Sound, Peary met with an accident. As the *Kite* reversed from some ice that she had been unable to break through, the rudder struck a heavy floe, slamming the heavy iron tiller to one side. Peary's leg was trapped against the wheelhouse, and broken. When their destination was reached, he was carried ashore strapped to a plank. The place is still known as Cripple Beach.

Some of the passengers wanted to turn back, but Dr Cook was able successfully to set the broken leg and Peary was confident of a speedy recovery. He ordered the *Kite* to press on, and asked for a compass in his cabin so that he could be certain his crew were obeying him. At McCormick Bay a wooden house was constructed according to Peary's design: twenty-one feet by twelve, with one room for the Pearys, another for the men's bunks. Four of the men were soon despatched to 'communicate with the natives':

I wished to become well acquainted with these most isolated and northerly of all peoples and, for the purposes of studying

this tribe, I hoped to induce not a few of them to spend the
winter months at or near our camp.

They were successfully induced with promises of wood (a rare commodity) and knives. Uppermost in Peary's mind was to learn not so much *about* them as *from* them – he needed to learn to drive dogs, to build igloos, to make clothes from the skins of seal, caribou, polar bear and musk ox. In particular he needed to know 'the location and ownership of every dog in the tribe, and also the financial rating of their owners – just what each one's possessions were; what each one most desired, and what would be most effective in bartering for the dogs'. The following summer's sledge journey would require the best in the tribe.

Henson set about building sledges according to another of Peary's new designs. The Eskimos had initially mistaken Henson for one of their own race, since he was clearly not a white man, and he became especially popular with them. He took to the art of dog-driving more quickly than the others, and was the only one in the party to learn more than a few words of Inuktitut, the Eskimo language.

The Eskimos were naturally curious to see Jo. One travelled many miles to satisfy his curiosity, and on being introduced to the Pearys asked, 'Which one is the woman?' Jo preferred to keep her distance:

I dislike very much to have the natives in my room, on account
of their dirty condition, and especially as they are alive with
parasites, of which I am in deadly fear . . .

Persuaded to visit an igloo, she was 'dismayed' to find the Eskimo women removed all their clothing as the temperature rose, 'just as unconcernedly as though no one were present'.

Peary and Cook, on the other hand, found the subjects of their 'ethnological' photographs more reluctant to disrobe for the camera. 'They could not understand at first why I desired to take their photographs in a nude condition,' wrote Peary, 'and I am not sure that they ever got a very clear idea of the matter.' He handled the camera while Cook posed the subjects and recorded a variety of measurements. In this way seventy-five Eskimos from the tribe were photographed for the benefit of science.

The long dark winter passed as the party made their preparations for the difficult journey to come. Only Verhoeff showed signs of strain. He had been given a stern dressing-down by Peary when he made an unauthorised excursion from the camp. A 500-yard limit was imposed for the winter, in the interests of safety, and Peary did not like to see any rule he made flouted. Verhoeff brooded on this and grew resentful, not only of Peary, but of his wife. During his watch he would deliberately keep the fire low in order to make her shiver.

The crossing of the ice cap began on 3 May. Peary chose five men for the sledging party. Henson was quickly disabled by a frozen heel, and sent back. Cook and Gibson accompanied Peary until 24 May. Thereafter, Peary and Astrup were on their own. Some of the dogs died, a sledge broke, deep snowdrifts slowed their progress, and a blizzard stopped them altogether for three days. But they forced themselves on.

Back at McCormick Bay, Jo and the rest of the party grew more anxious with each passing week. On 24 July the *Kite* arrived to take the entire expedition home, but still there was no sign of Peary. The Eskimos muttered that he must be dead. By the first week of August they were beginning to run out of time: the channel would not remain navigable for much longer. And then suddenly, on 6 August, they appeared: emaciated, exhausted and exhilarated.

At the very limit of their range, some 600 miles from McCormick Bay, the plateau had unexpectedly dropped, in a 3800-foot cliff, to what he named Independence Bay:

> We stood upon the north-east coast of Greenland and, looking
> far over the surface of a mighty glacier on our right and through
> the broad mouth of the bay, we saw stretching away to the
> horizon the great ice fields of the Arctic Ocean . . . all our
> fatigues of six weeks' struggle over the ice cap were forgotten in
> the grandeur of that view.

The northern limit and insularity of Greenland was discovered. A channel seemed to run east to west, separating Greenland from a land to the north.

The mood of celebration on the *Kite* was cut short by the failure of Verhoeff to return from a two-day outing to collect mineral samples. Six days of searching failed to explain the mystery. Tracks were found near a glacier and it was presumed he had fallen into a crevasse. Leaving a cache of provisions behind, the *Kite* departed for New York and a tumultuous reception.

Peary returned to north-west Greenland in 1893–5, with Henson, a pregnant wife (Marie Peary was the first white baby to be born above the Arctic Circle) and a larger expedition. The plan was to retrace his route, add more detail to his discoveries and, to the excitement of his backers, seek a route to the Pole. The Second Greenland Expedition was as much a failure as the first had been a success. Though Independence Bay was reached once more, too many dogs had died and supplies were too low to proceed further. Peary and Henson returned in desperate condition, accompanied by a single dog of the sixty that had set out. Almost delirious in his fatigue, depressed by his failure, Peary dreamt Henson was trying to poison him.

The dream of an Imperial Highway to the Pole had turned sour, and now Peary returned to the plan he had favoured before setting foot in Greenland: through Smith Sound and the Kane Basin, a ship would force its way north between Greenland and Ellesmere Island. It might even be possible to repeat what the British explorer Nares had achieved in 1875 in the *Alert*: reach Cape Sheridan, on the shores of the Arctic Ocean itself. Here the party should wait, through several winters if necessary, for the best conditions in which to rush northward for the Pole.

The failure of the Second Greenland Expedition did not cause too much damage to Peary's reputation. He diverted public attention by bringing back three gigantic meteorites, which now stand in the American Museum of Natural History – the largest ever displayed. The 'iron mountain' had been the source of metal from which the Polar Eskimos fashioned tools. Captain John Ross had heard about an iron mountain during his first encounters with the tribe in 1818, but no white man before Peary had located it. The meteorites, one of which was estimated at 100 tons in weight, were both a popular and scientific success. With these tangible prizes he could muster support for a new expedition.

There were other 'prizes'. The museum was presented with – in fact, was sold – five barrels of Eskimo remains. In the same cargo were six living Eskimos. An eager public queued at the quayside to inspect them. Also destined for the museum, they were accommodated in its basement; here they quickly began to fall ill, unable as they were to cope with the diseases of the civilised world. By 1898 four were dead. It emerged later that the bodies of some of them were sent to the museum's macerating plant where the flesh was stripped and the bones prepared for exhibition.

The death of the Eskimos attracted much bad publicity, and Peary distanced himself from the matter. The millionaire president of the museum, Morris Jesup, had become his principal backer, and was pulling strings to form a 'Peary Arctic Club' of wealthy and patriotic businessmen dedicated to seeing the Stars and Stripes planted at the Pole. Members could expect to have newly discovered geographical features named after them.

The money was in place by early 1898, and, as a result of a personal appeal to President McKinley by one of Peary's friends, five years' leave from the Navy was granted. He had the time and the money, and he had a ship: the British press baron Lord Northcliffe had offered the *Windward*. This ship, and Peary's impatience, were to be his undoing, setting in motion a disastrous chain of events. The steam yacht needed new engines, and would have had them but for a machinists' strike in England. Without them she was 'practically nothing but a sailing craft', capable of only three and a half knots, and no match for the heavy ice of the Kane Basin. Peary could have delayed, but 'the lateness of the season was such that I had to make the most of the *Windward* as she was'. Behind his impatience was the anticipated presence of a competitor in the area: the Norwegian explorer Otto Sverdrup was known to be planning an expedition on the *Fram*. This Peary referred to, with wild exaggeration, as 'the appropriation of my plan and field of work'. He had come to regard the area as his domain, and other explorers were not welcome.

The *Windward* was able to proceed no further than Cape D'Urville in the Kane Basin. There she was beset by ice and the party forced to disembark more than 200 miles south of the latitudes he had hoped to reach. He had planned to winter in Greely's old base at Fort Conger, in readiness for an assault on the Pole. Peary's decision to risk the long sledge journey to Conger in the January moonlight of 1899 was apparently motivated by his fear that Sverdrup might beat him to it. The desperate journey left Peary permanently crippled from the effects of frostbite.

From that moment the expedition was doomed to failure, yet Peary simply refused to come home. In the autumn of 1899 he wrote to Jo:

You are right, dear, life is slipping away. That cannot come to you more forcibly than it has repeatedly to me in times of darkness and inaction the past year . . . But there is something beyond me, something outside of me, which impels me irresistibly to the work. I shall certainly come back to you. I believe I shall accomplish my object and then hand in hand we will meet the days until the end comes.

Increasingly anxious, his wife and young daughter Marie decided to come north with the *Windward* on her return to Greenland in the summer of 1900. They brought with them the news that Marie's baby sister, whom her father had never seen, had died. Again the ship was beset by ice in the Kane Basin. They were forced to winter at Payer Harbour while Peary, 300 miles to the north, beyond communication and unaware of their presence, settled in for the long Arctic night at Conger. Jo's misery was complete when one of Eskimo women who joined the *Windward* for the winter cheerfully related the story of her relationship with 'Pearyaksoah' ('Big Peary'); the child she carried was his. Allakasingwah was 'the belle of the tribe' in Peary's eyes. He had met her at another ethnological photograph session, during the Second Greenland Expedition, when she was ten years old and 'just beginning to develop into a woman'. She had been unusually reluctant to take her clothes off. 'You will be surprised, perhaps annoyed,' wrote Jo that winter, 'when you hear that I came up on a ship . . . but believe me had I known how things were with you here I should not have come.'

Peary received Jo's letters as he headed south from Conger the next spring, having aborted an attempt on the Pole after only eight days of marching. Soon they were reunited, having been apart for three years. Jo did not try to persuade him to return; she knew her husband was not capable of giving up the fight before a more serious attempt was made.

Back in New York, the Peary Arctic Club had been shaken by news of Peary's frostbite; now they were worried that the *Windward*, sent north to locate him, had not returned before the winter. A second relief ship, the *Erik*, was dispatched, with the club's secretary at the helm. It brought news that Peary's mother had died. 'Before she went away,' the letter told him, 'she felt sure you were no longer living, and I think a part of her life went out at that time.' He was inconsolable.

At the club's request, Peary's former colleague Dr Cook was on board the *Erik*, charged with examining Peary and making a report on his health.

> *The first impression was of an iron man, wrecked in ambition, wrecked in physique, wrecked in hope. To the public he was on the way to reach the Pole, but to himself, no such effort had been made. Peary was worried, anxious, discouraged as I had never seen him before.*

Peary knew he would not be successful, yet the ships were sent home without him. He was compelled to return for one more battle with the pack ice; only there would he accept his inevitable defeat.

Just to reach the shores of the Arctic Ocean from their winter station at Payer Harbour, Peary, Henson and seven Eskimos travelled 400 miles in temperatures of below -35°C, knowing the hardest part of the journey was still to come. Their tortuous progress over the jagged ice, held up by blizzards and areas of open water, realised just 81 miles in 18 days. Here, more than 300 miles from the Pole, Peary threw in the towel. The position of their final camp was an American record for Farthest North, but there was no celebration. 'The game is off,' he wrote in his diary. 'My dream of sixteen years is ended. I cannot accomplish the impossible.'

During the long retreat to a last rendezvous with the *Windward*, Peary reflected bitterly on four years of failure.

> *Now a maimed old man, unsuccessful after the most arduous work, away from wife and child, mother dead, one baby dead. Has the game been worth the candle? And yet I could not have done otherwise than stick to it.*

By the time the *Windward* reached New York, his mood had lightened, and a remarkable transformation was under way. Uncharacteristically, he wrote only the briefest report on the expedition, as if to close the door on it. Everything that could have been done to make it successful had been done, he concluded; he had been handicapped by his ship's inability to place his base camp further north and by poor conditions on the pack ice. He declared himself as strong as ever in his belief that the Pole could be attained via the Smith Sound route, 'that it ought to be done and must be secured for this country'. He told his backers he was more than willing to try again, but this time a special ship must be built capable of smashing its way to the edge of the Polar Sea.

While Peary persuaded them to continue their support, another admirer was beginning his term as President of the United States. Theodore Roosevelt had followed Peary's exploits with great interest for many years. He liked the explorer's machismo, his grim determination, his bluntness and his patriotism. They were qualities Roosevelt liked to see in himself. Peary in turn would call Roosevelt 'the most intensely vital man, and the biggest man, America has ever produced'. With the public endorsement of the president, preparations for a new expedition gathered pace.

Peary designed and personally supervised the construction of a new ship, named, with some inevitability, the *Roosevelt*. She was small enough, at 184 feet, to be easily manoeuvred amongst the floes and bergs. Broad of beam, she was built of wood so that her hull could flex slightly under pressure, and be easily repaired; steel girders were installed to prevent her from being crushed altogether by the ice. The curve of her hull was such that when the ice squeezed her, she would rise up, and then break through the ice beneath her with her weight. Most important of all, she was fitted with a massive steam engine, driving a propeller more than eleven feet across.

It proved to be a brilliant design: the *Roosevelt* not only penetrated Smith Sound and the Kane Basin, but continued to ram her way through the narrow channels until she had reached a new northerly record for a ship under its own power. There had been close calls along the way when the ice held her, causing the deck to bulge and the rigging to sag, but in September 1905 she delivered Peary to the wintering position he wanted, on the edge of the Arctic Ocean.

From his failure in 1902 Peary had learned that a single party heading out across the pack ice could not sustain itself for the many weeks it would take to reach the Pole and return to land. This time he used a system of supporting sledge 'divisions' to relay supplies behind the trail-breaking party and, it was hoped, keep the return trail open through the ice hummocks and around the 'leads' of open water.

At the 'Big Lead', just beyond 84° N, the expedition came to a standstill, confronted by a wide expanse of open water. The rear sledge divisions caught up and soon all were camped at the water's edge. Six days passed before the water froze sufficiently to allow a crossing, but immediately a furious blizzard forced them to camp and wait a second time. The relay system had broken down, and while they waited at the Big Lead the eastward drift of the pack ice swept them away from the return trail. Peary was still eighty miles short of the world record Farthest North set by the Italian Duke of Abruzzi's expedition. To proceed was to take the risk of the Big Lead blocking his return to land; to go back now, without even the record, would have meant utter failure and the end of his dream. The sledge divisions were sent back, while Peary, Henson and four Eskimos, their surplus equipment abandoned, began a dash towards the Pole.

A new Farthest North was reached, but only just: Peary's 87° 6' N beat the Italian record by a mere thirty-two miles. A flag was planted and photographs taken, but no camp made. The whole party was by now exhausted, supplies dangerously low, the dogs weakening. They began the long and agonising journey to land. Sledges were broken for fuel with which the weakest of the dogs were cooked. The Big Lead was crossed on a thin film of ice that buckled underneath them as they slowly edged forward 'in silence, each man busy with his thoughts'.

On reaching the Greenland coast, they came across one of the supporting sledge parties, hopelessly lost and so close to death from starvation that they had already eaten their spare sealskin boots. Had Peary not found musk oxen, both parties would have perished. Knowing his life depended on it, Peary took several moments to steady himself before shooting.

The beating of the record was 'but an empty bauble compared with the splendid jewel on which I had set my heart for years'. He needed something else to prove the worth of the expedition. After a short period of recuperation on the *Roosevelt* he set off along the unexplored coast of northern Ellesmere, naming features after the members of the Peary Arctic Club:

> *What I see before me in all its splendid, sunlit savageness, is mine, mine by the right of discovery, to be credited to me, and associated with my name, generations after I have ceased to be.*

Even before the *Roosevelt* sailed for home, Peary was planning a return in the following spring, but she had been so badly damaged at her winter mooring that a year's delay was required for repairs. There was time to receive plaudits for his Farthest North. At the annual banquet of the National Geographic Society in 1906 he was presented with the Hubbard Medal by President Roosevelt, who praised his 'courage and hardihood'. Accepting the award, Peary preferred to speak of his future conquest of the Pole. He used words that did not try to disguise his obsession: 'it is the thing which should be done for the honour and credit of this country, the thing which it is intended that I should do, and the thing that I must do'.

He was not unduly concerned when he learned that his old colleague Dr Frederick Cook, in Greenland on what was ostensibly a hunting trip, was claiming to have discovered a new route to the Pole. Since his association with Peary, Cook had made a reputation for himself on board the first ship to winter in Antarctica, and as conqueror of Mount McKinley in Alaska, the highest peak in North America. In polar clubs and geographical societies there were rumours that his claim to Mount McKinley was a fraud, and now Peary's friends warned him that Cook might try to get away with something more outrageous in the Arctic. Peary was annoyed, of course, to hear another explorer was in 'his' territory, but he did not consider Cook's 'new route', beginning at a more southerly latitude, to have any chance of success. He dismissed the suggestion of a hoax as an absurdity and continued his preparations.

When the *Roosevelt* left New York for the Arctic on 6 July 1908 (a stifling day, incidentally, on which thirteen New Yorkers died of the heat) Peary knew that he was going north for the last time. It was 'the last arrow in the quiver'. At fifty-two his body would no longer do whatever his will required of it. Nevertheless he was confident in his experience, his plan and the team he had assembled.

There were old hands, and tenderfeet. Henson had been a member of all his major expeditions and was by now as good a dog-driver and hunter as the best of the Eskimos. Only he was fluent in Inuktitut. Though he was still required to address Peary as 'sir' in the field, Peary conceded that he 'couldn't do without him'. Captain Robert Bartlett was master of the *Roosevelt*, and after Henson the most important man in Peary's plans. A burly, tireless, high-spirited Newfoundlander, he had brought the damaged *Roosevelt* home in the most difficult circumstances in 1906, and was on his way to becoming the outstanding Arctic sea captain of the period.

George Wardwell, the chief engineer, John Murphy, the boatswain, and the young Professor Ross Marvin were also veterans of the 1906 expedition. Three men were making their debut in the Arctic: Donald MacMillan, a teacher, John Goodsell, the expedition surgeon, and George Borup, just one year out of Yale, where he had made a reputation as a wrestler. All were to play important parts on the ice the next spring.

At Cape York the *Roosevelt* received the familiar welcome from the Eskimos, their sealskin kayaks surrounding the ship. Peary referred to them as 'my Eskimos' and frequently characterised them as children, 'easily elated, easily discouraged'. He portrayed himself as their benefactor:

> *I have grown to love this simple, childlike people . . . every individual is known to me . . . as thoroughly as the patients of an old-fashioned family physician are known to him, and the feeling existing between us is not so very different.*
>   *The things I have given them are absolutely out of their world, as far beyond their own unaided efforts as the moon and Mars are beyond the dwellers of this planet.*

With wood, knives, saws and rifles, Peary once more set about bartering for their dogs and selecting the 'pick and flower' of the hunters in the tribe. To the Eskimos, 'Pearyaksoah's' determination to travel far out on the treacherous sea ice was difficult to understand. There was no food out there, and a good chance of drowning or starving or freezing to death. But they well understood the rewards that would come at the end of the expedition.

The *Roosevelt* proceeded to Etah. Here they were approached by a strange white man: sick, dishevelled, tearful, he begged to be given passage home. Rudolph Franke had been Dr Frederick Cook's single white companion. Cook had gone northwards with his Eskimos the previous summer, leaving Franke in charge of his hut and giving him permission to return to America if he could find a whaling ship to take him. After a winter with the Eskimos at Etah, he was in Dr Goodsell's opinion suffering from scurvy and was 'in a serious mental state'. 'That is an example,' Peary warned his party, 'of what can happen to a white man in the Arctic.' Reluctantly, Peary agreed to give Franke a passage home on his supply ship, the *Erik*, on the condition that all of Cook's fox skins and narwhal tusks were turned over to him.

Having taken aboard 246 dogs, 22 Eskimo men, 17 women, 10 children, 70 tons of whale meat and 50 of walrus, the *Roosevelt* once more butted and rammed her way north to Cape Sheridan, arriving on the same day, within fifteen minutes of the exact time she had arrived in 1905. A string of caches was immediately laid to Cape Columbia, the chosen starting point, ninety miles to the west. Through the long dark winter the ship bustled with activity as sledges were made, furs sewn and sledge rations calculated. Hunting parties made use of the moonlight. Nearly a hundred Arctic hares were killed by simply walking up to them and clubbing them with rifle butts. Never having seen a human, they hadn't learnt to run away.

In February the sledge divisions made their way to Cape Columbia, and on 1 March the procession of 24 men, 19 sledges and 133 dogs moved noiselessly on to the pack ice. Barlett broke the trail, while Peary travelled at the rear. The weather was relatively warm, making travelling more tolerable but increasing the chances of open water on the trail. After four marches they saw 'a broad and ominous band of black' on the horizon: the vapour clouds marking the Big Lead. They were held up for six nervous days of 'intolerable inaction'. Two of the older Eskimos pretended to be sick and were immediately sent back by Peary with a written message to the mate of the *Roosevelt* describing the treatment they and their families should receive: they would have to make their own way back to Greenland.

According to the plan Borup and Marvin were to relay supplies from Cape Columbia to the advance party, but were themselves held up by a lead close to the shore. When the Big Lead closed Peary decided to wait no longer for them and the vital fuel on their sledges, taking a chance on their catching up. On 14 March, to his great relief, he saw Marvin's party chasing him down, 'men and dogs steaming like a squadron of battleships'.

The weather was now colder and the going faster. One by one the sledge divisions were sent back to land. Goodsell's division was the first to return, at 84° 29' N. MacMillan was next, suffering from a frozen heel. Five marches later, Borup returned from his farthest north, at 85° 50' N, his 'bright young face slightly clouded with regret'. Peary had not told the men how far each of them would be required to go. On 26 March, having made a good fifty miles in the last three marches, it was Marvin's turn to retreat. The young tenderfoot had reached 86° 38' N. That day a 'strange and melancholy light' made Peary feel uneasy.

A few miles short of the 88th parallel Peary sent back Bartlett – the last of his supporting divisions. The tough Newfoundlander had done most of the trail-breaking and wanted to go all the way to the Pole, now only 133 miles from their camp. Peary chose Henson for the final dash. That Peary doubted Henson's ability to lead a returning division safely to land was one reason for taking him. Another was that he was black. Peary freely admitted that he wanted to be the only white man at the North Pole.

A little after midnight on 2 April Peary, Henson, and the Eskimos Egingwah, Seegloo, Ootah and Ooqueah set out from 'Camp Bartlett'. For the first time Peary, feeling 'the keenest exhilaration . . . even exultation', broke trail. The ice conditions improved, and with the weather holding they were able to reel off the miles at a rate of more then twenty per march. At one stage they were able to travel on the smooth ice of a frozen lead and the dogs broke into a gallop. 'My pulse beat high,' Peary wrote, 'for the breath of success seemed already in my nostrils.' At the end of the fifth march from Camp Bartlett, at ten o'clock in the morning of 6 April 1909, Peary took a latitude sighting that gave their position as 89° 57' N. They had reached the vicinity of the Pole. His life's purpose had been achieved.

Henson approached Peary to congratulate him, but he turned away, both hands covering his face. He felt nothing but sudden and overwhelming exhaustion. As a young man he had once said that the fame of Columbus could only be matched by 'him who shall one day stand with 360 degrees of longitude beneath his motionless foot, and for whom East and West shall have vanished'. Now that he had reached the place he was unable to absorb its significance: 'I cannot bring myself to realise it,' he wrote, 'it all seems so simple and so commonplace.' To Ootah, the ice looked very much like the ice back at home.

Somewhat revived by a short sleep, Peary composed a short triumphal entry for his field diary: 'The Pole at last!!! The prize of three centuries, my dream and ambition for twenty-three years. *Mine* at last . . .' To complete the work, he sledged ten miles on, where another set of observations told him he had gone beyond the Pole, having travelled first north and then south without changing direction. More short journeys and a series of observations satisfied him that, although the limitations of his instruments made the precise spot impossible to determine, the Pole was somewhere within the small area he had covered. Now he could celebrate: five flags were planted, the Eskimos posed for a series of photographs, and a message was deposited in the ice. In it Peary not only recorded their arrival at the Pole but stated that he had 'formally taken possession of the entire region, and adjacent, for and in the name of the President of the United States of America'. After thirty-six hours at the North Pole camp, they began the 413-mile journey back to land.

I did not wait for any lingering farewell of my life's goal . . . one backward glance I gave – then turned my face toward the south and toward the future.

The future contained his worst nightmare. When Peary telegraphed to the world news of his triumph, Dr Frederick Cook was at a banquet in Copenhagen, celebrating his discovery, on 21 April 1908, of the North Pole.

Chapter Three

THE SLIPPERY POLE

D r Cook possessed in abundance the quality that Peary, as a young man, had tried and failed to acquire: personal charisma. Even Peary had liked him. When the Brooklyn physician made his debut as an explorer on Peary's first Greenland expedition of 1891, he was singled out for praise in the leader's report: 'Personally I owe much to his professional skill, and unruffled patience and coolness in an emergency . . .' He set Peary's broken leg, and supported him in his determination to press on when many in the party had taken fright and were ready to turn back. One night on the ice cap the two men had huddled together in a snow hole waiting for a blizzard to pass; Peary had placed his trousers on Cook's head to keep him warm. The doctor was invited to return to Greenland on the second expedition, but withdrew when Peary refused him permission to publish an article about the Eskimos in a magazine. Peary never waived his right, established in a standard contract, to be the sole publisher of any article based on his expeditions. According to Cook, it was a 'friendly' parting of the ways. Peary was the more disappointed of the two.

In 1898, while Peary was beginning a fruitless four-year expedition in the Arctic, Cook put the maximum distance between them by joining a Belgian expedition to Antarctica. A late replacement for a Dutch physician who had suddenly got cold feet, Cook made the most of his opportunity on the *Belgica*. Among those he impressed was one Roald Amundsen, the ship's mate. Then twenty-five years old and on his first major expedition, the laconic Norwegian would accumulate more Polar honours than any man in history: first to navigate the Northwest Passage, first to stand at the South Pole, first, in all probability, to fly over the North Pole. When the *Belgica* was beset by ice in the Bellingshausen Sea, Amundsen, Cook and her crew became the first men to spend a winter below the Antarctic Circle. They were facing entrapment for a second 'Antarctic night' until Cook's plan – the sawing of a thousand-yard channel through the ice to the nearest area of open water – liberated the ship. But it was the role Cook played on the *Belgica* through the long, dark polar winter, when her crew suffered from scurvy, hunger, and in some cases madness, that won Amundsen's praise:

> *It was in this fearful emergency, during these thirteen long months in which almost the certainty of death stared us steadily in the face, that I came to know Dr Cook intimately . . . He, of all the ship's company, was the one man of unfaltering courage, unfailing hope, endless cheerfulness, and unwearied kindness. When anyone was sick, he was at his bedside to comfort him; when any was disheartened, he was there to encourage and inspire. And not only was his faith undaunted, but his ingenuity and enterprise were boundless.*

Minor improvisations included wrapping a sledge in penguin skin to reduce friction (feather side out), and persuading the men to stand half-naked in front of the roaring furnace to compensate for the lack of sun. In his diary he meticulously recorded every detail of the Polar experience, from the taste of the penguins he clubbed to death with his ski pole (like fishy liver), to the effect of the long night on the growth-rate of his hair and the condition of his fingernails ('the skin around the nails has a tendency to creep over them'). He took a series of beautiful photographs of the *Belgica* using ninety-minute exposures in the Antarctic moonlight.

Cook became a hero in Belgium. He was knighted by King Leopold I in 1899, and awarded the Gold Medal of the Royal Belgian Academy of Sciences and the silver medal of the Royal Geographical Society of Belgium. He returned briefly to his medical practice until, at the request of the Peary Arctic Club, he joined the relief expedition in search of Peary, who had been in the Arctic for three years and was known to have lost his toes. The doctor's prognosis, that Peary was finished as an Arctic traveller, proved to be wide of the mark.

Cook made the giant leap from Belgian hero to American hero by way of Mount McKinley in Alaska. The highest mountain on the North American continent, at 20,300 feet, is known today as Mount Denali.

'The most Arctic of the big mountains of the world' was unclimbed, the brutal landscape to its east entirely unexplored. Although he had no mountaineering experience, Cook fancied his chances and, in 1903, organised an expedition to attempt the summit. It failed, but a remarkable circumnavigation of the range was completed. Three years later he returned to try again. On 3 October 1906 the *New York Times* reported his unexpected success, and the geographical societies of America prepared to welcome a new star. On his return he was offered the presidency of the Explorers' Club of New York, succeeding Major-General Greely, and in December, at the prestigious annual banquet of the National Geographic Society, he shared top billing with Peary. While Peary received a medal for his Farthest North, Cook was praised by Alexander Graham Bell: 'the only American who has explored both extremes of the world' had now 'been to the top of the American continent'. It was clear that Cook shared Peary's appetite for fame. Discreetly, he made up his mind to challenge Peary for 'the last great geographical prize'.

There was no Arctic Club of millionaires to support Cook, and there might have been no challenge but for a stroke of luck. While Peary's *Roosevelt* was being refitted for his final expedition, Cook met John R. Bradley. The wealthy big-game hunter was looking for a man who could take him to the area of Smith Sound, where he planned to shoot polar bears. Cook had a proposal to make, and Bradley, though initially nervous, was soon persuaded to collaborate. It was agreed that the expedition would be fitted in secret with the equipment Cook needed for an attempt on the Pole. There was nothing to lose, the doctor coaxed: if conditions proved unfavourable, they would return quietly, as if from a normal hunting trip.

Bradley was happy to leave the preparations to his new associate: Cook seemed to know what he was doing. A schooner was bought and renamed in honour of the man writing the cheques. Within a few weeks, the *John R. Bradley*'s engine was replaced and her hull strengthened for the ice. To allow for the possibility of ice-entrapment, two years of supplies were loaded. A thousand pounds of the sledging ration pemmican, and a quantity of hickory for the construction of sledges comprised the bulk of Cook's special equipment. As the *Bradley* was made ready for her 'hunting trip', Cook found time to make casual visits to the dock where the *Roosevelt* was being refitted, somewhat behind schedule, and seek advice from her captain on matters of ice navigation. The *Bradley* left Gloucester, Massachusetts, on 3 July 1907. The *Roosevelt*'s departure was postponed for another year.

'No man possessing a sense of honour would be guilty' of what Cook had done, Peary fumed in a letter to the *New York Times*. He had just heard from the Explorers' Club that Cook, by now in Greenland, was preparing for an attempt on the Pole by a new route. Though Peary did not believe Cook could succeed, he feared his rival would take the best dogs from the Eskimos. The Explorers' Club now decided to offer Peary the vacant position of its President. He accepted, but made it a condition that 'in the event of Dr Cook returning and claiming to have found the North Pole, proper proofs would be demanded of him'.

Peary reached Greenland on his way north in August 1908. At Etah he learned that Cook had set out six months earlier from the nearby settlement of Annoatok, with Rudolph Franke, his only white companion, ten Eskimos, eleven sledges and 105 dogs. Peary was aware of Cook's plan to travel west across Ellesmere and north along the ice of Eureka Sound, before striking out across the frozen ocean towards the Pole. Franke and the supporting parties had turned back in March; of the doctor, who had elected to press on with just two of the Eskimos, a couple of sledges, and twenty-six dogs, there had been no word since. Not only did Peary believe the attainment of the Pole by so small an expedition, beginning at such a latitude, to be an absolute impossibility, he was also certain that Cook – since he had not returned by August – must have starved or frozen to death. What did Cook know of travelling on the pack ice? Peary, with all his resources and experience, had nearly died during his last attempt to cross it. There was no doubt in his mind. Before he took the *Roosevelt* north, he nailed a notice to the door of Cook's hut:

> This house belongs to Dr F A Cook, but Dr Cook is long ago
> dead and there is no use to search for him. Therefore, I,
> Commander Robert E Peary, install my boatswain in this
> deserted house.

When winter came to Annoatok, it seemed Peary must have been right: without a ship or a hut, how could Cook and the two Eskimos survive the cold and constant darkness of the long Arctic night? If they had been alive, they would surely have returned before winter. But on 18 April 1909 the Eskimos of Annoatok saw three figures, without sledges or dogs, stumbling towards their igloos. Half starved, caked in dirt, hair to their shoulders, they were not immediately recognised as the men who had been given up for dead. Harry Whitney, a hunter who had travelled to Etah on Peary's support ship, was with the Eskimos who rushed to greet them: 'You have been away fourteen months with food for two months,' he said. 'How have you done this?'

And where had they been? Cook told an astonished Whitney that they had reached the North Pole almost a year before, on 21 April 1908. He also told him that he should keep the news to himself. If Peary returned from the north, he should tell him only that his Farthest North record of 1906 had been beaten. The Eskimos, too, were instructed to tell no one. Cook wanted to break the news to the civilised world in person.

He had a remarkable tale to tell. The expedition had travelled as planned across Smith Sound and the narrowest part of Ellesmere Island, before heading north, between Ellesmere and Axel Heiberg Island. These proved to be good hunting grounds, as Cook had reason to believe they would be from the accounts of the Norwegian explorer Otto Sverdrup. The men and dogs fed well on polar bears and musk oxen. Expecting to return by the same route, caches of food were laid at fifty-mile intervals. They reached the northern tip of Axel Heiberg Island in mid-March. High above them on the cliffs at Cape Thomas Hubbard they saw a cairn built by Peary to mark the western limit of his exploration in 1906.

From this desolate vantage point, some 520 miles of moving sea ice stretched out towards the North Pole. Whatever food they needed would have to be carried on their sledges. Cook initially took to the sea ice with four men, fifty-four dogs and two heavy sledges. After fifty miles he decided to send two of the Eskimos back, proceeding with just twenty-six dogs and two sledges. According to Cook's story, they advanced steadily, at an average of fifteen miles a day. There were moments of great danger. The Big Lead, some two miles wide at that point, had a thin coating of ice:

A dangerous cracking sound pealed in every direction under my feet . . . With every tread the thin sheet ice perceptibly sank under me, and waved, in small billows, like a sheet of rubber. Stealthily, as though we were trying to filch some victory, we crept forward . . .

One night a lead opened directly beneath the igloo in which Cook was sleeping:

Out of the blankness of sleep . . . I heard beneath me a series of echoing, thundering noises . . . I saw the dome of the snowhouse open above me . . . I think I tried to rise, when suddenly everything seemed lifted from under me; I experienced the suffocating sense of falling, and next . . . felt about my body a terrific tightening pressure like that of a chilled and closing shell of steel, driving the life and breath from me.

When the Eskimos pulled him out of the water a few seconds later, his reindeer-skin sleeping bag was already sheathed in ice, yet when they beat it off the skin was found to be perfectly dry. Etukishook and Ahwelah accompanied Cook for the promised reward of a gun and a knife each.

Cook claimed the discovery not only of the Pole, but of a new land. By 1907 most of the circumpolar coast had been mapped, but it was not known whether any land mass existed within the Arctic basin. On 30 March, some 220 miles north of Cape Thomas Hubbard, Cook believed he could see a land mass on the western horizon. Through his telescope, the coast of 'Bradley Land' appeared to extend for at least fifty miles. It was a considerable distance away, and as their rations were limited, no detour was made to set foot on it.

On 21 April 1908 Cook determined that they had reached the North Pole, obtaining a fix 'with the sextant and accessory instruments like those used by shipmasters'. Dead reckoning of the distance covered from Cape Thomas Hubbard supported his calculation. As astronomers predicted, the sun appeared to circle the horizon at a constant height. Cook measured his shadow at hourly intervals from a fixed point, and found that it remained the same. The Eskimos watched impassively as Cook shouted and danced in celebration. Cook's description of what he liked to call the 'Boreal Centre' is almost hallucinatory:

*I felt the glory which the prophet feels in his vision, with which
the poet thrills in his dream. About the frozen plains my
imagination evoked aspects of grandeur. I saw silver and crystal
palaces, such as were never built by man, with turrets flaunting
. . . the shifting mirages seemed like the ghosts of dead armies,
magnified and transfigured, huge and spectral.*

Cook hoped to return to the caches he had deposited in February and
March, but the ice drift took them far to the west: they reached land at
the Rignes Islands, just as their supplies ran out. An inventory of their
remaining supplies and equipment was gloomily made: silk tent, col-
lapsible canvas boat, two sledges, two rifles, a hundred rounds of
ammunition, knives, an oil lamp (no oil), 710 matches and a few tins of
pemmican. Eleven dogs were left of the twenty-six. Cook calculated that
they were at least 600 miles from the nearest human being, 'even
savage Eskimos or Indians'. If they were to survive they would have to
return to the Stone Age.

Travelling east towards Greenland, against the ice current, was
impossible. Cook chose instead to drift with the ice moving southward
in the hope of finding a whaling ship in Lancaster Sound. In many areas
they found the summer game to be so plentiful that the Eskimos were
reluctant to move on. Derelict stone dwellings and litterings of animal
bones were evidence of successful Eskimo habitation some time in the
past. But winter was coming. At the western mouth of Jones Sound they
abandoned their dogs and one of the sledges and took to the tiny canvas
boat. The dogs, Cook hoped, would join the wolf packs.

The boat was holed by jags of ice, and once by the white tusk of a
walrus; on each occasion they made for the nearest ice-floe, hauled the
boat from the water and repaired the damage with hide cut from their
boots. When they reached Cape Sparbo, on North Devon Island, the site
of an ancient Eskimo village now partly submerged beneath the water,
it was early September. They had four cartridges left, and half a sledge.
Their clothing was in shreds. It was decided to spend the winter here, in
a tiny cave, its narrow entrance covered by the remains of their tent.
Hares were killed with slingshot and snares, musk oxen with stones and
lances. Winter supplies of meat and blubber were cached. During the
long months of darkness they were tyrannised by marauding polar
bears:

*We were not permitted beyond an enclosed hundred feet from
the hole of our den. Not an inch of ground or a morsel of food
was permitted us without a contest . . . Occasionally we
ventured out to deliver a lance . . . in other cases we shot arrows
through the peep-hole. A bear head again would burst through
the silk-covered window near the roof, where knives, at close
range and in good light, could be driven with sweet vengeance.*

On 18 February 1909, a few days after the polar dawn, they began the
long walk north-eastwards to Annoatok. By the time Whitney greeted
them exactly two months later, the three 'wildest of wild men' had eaten
their boots and 'other things not to be mentioned'. Despite his weakened
condition, Cook allowed himself only three days of eating, sleeping and
washing (he scrubbed himself 'by instalments') before beginning a 700-
mile sledge journey south to Upernavik, where he hoped to find a ship
bound either for the United States or for Copenhagen. He was determined to tell his story to the world at the first opportunity. Much of his
property, including his instruments and some of his original observations, he entrusted to Whitney to bring back with him to New York.

Cook was aboard the blubber ship *Hans Egede*, en route for
Denmark, when Peary's *Roosevelt* reached Etah on its triumphant journey homeward. He had already heard from the Eskimos that Cook had
returned that spring from Jones Sound; now he learned that Cook was
claiming to have reached the North Pole, a full year ahead of him. On
board the *Roosevelt* the news was met with incredulity, then mirth.
According to his captain, Bob Bartlett, Peary was 'not especially concerned. He and I with our years of Arctic experience knew how utterly
impossible it was for Cook to have crossed a thousand miles of Polar
Sea ice without supporting parties.' Henson recalled thinking 'such a
story was so ridiculous and absurd that we simply laughed at it'.

Nevertheless Peary ordered the formal questioning of the two
Eskimos who accompanied Cook. Everything Etukishook and Ahwelah
said was to be written down. They told Peary's men that they had made
only three marches on the pack ice north of Axel Heiberg Island, and
never lost sight of land. According to Peary, 'Dr Cook had threatened
them if they should tell anything.' Armed with the testimony of the
Eskimos, Peary was confident that should anyone take Cook's claim
seriously, he would soon disabuse them.

Meanwhile, the ship on which Harry Whitney had hoped to return to the New York had not arrived. Fearing he could be marooned for a second winter with the Eskimos, he asked Peary for a berth on the *Roosevelt*; this Peary granted on the condition he brought none of Cook's effects with him. When he tried to smuggle the instruments and papers aboard amongst his own possessions, the ruse was discovered, and they were taken ashore to be buried under a pile of stones.

The *Hans Egede*, en route for Copenhagen, reached Lerwick in the Shetland Islands on 1 September. From here Cook telegraphed the Brussels Observatory and the *New York Herald*: 'Reached North Pole April 21st, 1908. Discovered land far north . . .' An American public waiting for word of Peary's final Polar expedition was stunned. The famous old war-horse had been beaten to the Pole by a fellow country-man of utterly contrasting style. There had been no razzmatazz at the quayside for Cook's departure, no presidential endorsements, no club of millionaires. In Copenhagen vast hat-waving crowds swarmed to the docks as Cook's boat approached. The scale of the welcome he received took Cook by surprise. The Crown Prince of Denmark stepped on to his boat to shake his hand. More than a hundred journalists had converged on the city. Most of them were impressed by Cook's modest demeanour, but one of them, Philip Gibbs of the London *Daily Chronicle*, said 'I never saw guilt and fear written more clearly on any human face.'

Cook was guest of honour at a formal dinner in Copenhagen, given by a newspaper for the visiting correspondents of the world, when the news arrived that Peary had 'nailed the Stars and Stripes to the Pole'. A note was passed to Cook and an announcement made to the assembled journalists. The hall was in uproar. Cook rose to his feet, expressed his pleasure at Peary's deserved achievement, and declared there was glory enough for all.

In Labrador, Peary received telegrams describing the events of the past week. He was astonished, and then horrified as he began to realise that the world accepted Cook's story: the glory he had spent his life winning was being accorded to a man he *knew* could not have done what he claimed. There was no delay from Peary in setting the record straight and no attempt to moderate his language. He telegraphed the New York papers, calling Cook a liar. 'I am the only white man who has ever reached the Pole,' he said. 'Cook has simply handed the public a gold brick.'

For the American newspapers it was the story of the decade. After so many failed expeditions, and so many deaths in attempting to reach the North Pole over the last hundred years, two Americans were claiming within a week of each other to be its discoverer. Better still, one was calling the other a fraud. For Peary, his hasty denunciation of Cook was a public relations disaster: he was perceived as a bad loser, the more so in the light of his rival's impeccable good manners. His wife pleaded with him to be more temperate, but the damage was done. A Pittsburgh newspaper poll recorded ninety-six per cent of its readership siding with the likeable Cook. Worse for Peary, many registered their belief that *he* was lying about his own journey to the Pole. An excited crowd welcomed Cook to Brooklyn when he returned from Copenhagen in late September. 'We Believe You' the banners exclaimed.

Cook now set to work on the preparation of his expedition data for submission to the University of Copenhagen; an expert commission there, he said, would confirm their validity. News of what had happened to Cook's instruments and some of his papers at the hands of Peary caused the shadow that had been cast over his reputation to darken a little further. He retired to his beloved island home, in Maine, in a confusion of despair and rage:

> *I have put my life into the effort to accomplish something which seemed to me a thing worth doing, and because it had the great attraction of being a clean, manly proposition. I pulled the thing off finally, and then have the whole matter soiled and smirched by a cowardly cur of a sordid imposter; am blackguarded by my own people because I attempt to warn them and keep them from making damned fools of themselves.*

The Peary Arctic Club, however, was working hard to expose Cook. Rumours that a hoax had been perpetrated on Mount McKinley in 1906 were investigated. By mid-October they were ready to deliver two hammer blows. The *New York Times* published the account given by Cook's two Eskimos in which they stated that they had never lost sight of land. But Cook's defence seemed plausible: the Eskimos would tell a white man whatever they believed he wanted to hear, especially such an intimidating man as Peary.

The next day's *New York Globe and Commercial Advertiser*

contained a sensational and far more damaging report: it included a sworn affidavit from Edward Barrill, Cook's companion on the McKinley expedition. It stated that they were never closer to the summit than a distance of fourteen miles, that the summit photograph was a fake, taken on an 8000-foot peak, and that his own diary had been 'doctored' on Cook's orders.

Cook tried to stand firm. Barrill had been bribed, he said; he would organise another expedition to the summit of McKinley to recover the documents he had cached there. But the tide of public opinion was turning against him. From the University of Copenhagen he asked for more time to prepare his expedition data, and from the Explorers' Club of New York time to assemble his McKinley records. The sang-froid he had displayed in Copenhagen disappeared; he became agitated, and tried to evade the relentless attentions of journalists and the Peary Arctic Club's private detectives whom he believed – apparently with good reason – were following his every move. 'On every side I sensed hostility,' he wrote, 'the sight of crowds filled me with a growing sort of terror.' On 24 November he shaved off his moustache, cut his hair short and fled New York. The disguise was completed with a black slouch hat.

Inevitably, Cook's disappearance was interpreted in many quarters as an admission of guilt. On 8 December his secretary arrived in Copenhagen with his North Pole records. The Peary Arctic Club had been waiting to play another card: the very next day the *New York Times* printed the affidavits of two rather dubious mariners, by the names of George Dunkle and August Loose. In their statements it was claimed Cook had offered to pay $2500 for help in fabricating navigational observations for his dash to the Pole. Furthermore, their statements suggested Cook did not even know how to make the longitudinal observations that would have told him he was at the Pole. He had seemed nervous to them; they had felt sorry for him, but not sorry enough to stop them selling their story. Again, the allegations were denied in a statement from Cook's secretary: Dunkle and Loose had been hired only to check through his navigational data. None of their calculations were included in his report. By now the newspapers were speculating whether Cook was 'the greatest and at the same time the stupidest charlatan' or the victim of 'the most malignant and devilishly ingenious persecution that hatred and envy could devise'.

The Copenhagen University Commission delivered its verdict on 21

December 1909: 'The material transmitted for examination contains no proof whatsoever that Dr Cook reached the North Pole.' They had received nothing more substantial than what Cook had already serialised in the *New York Herald*. Cook was lying low in Europe when the *New York Times* printed the headline: 'COOK'S CLAIM TO DISCOVERY OF NORTH POLE REJECTED; OUTRAGED DENMARK CALLS HIM A DELIBERATE SWINDLER'.

The days when an explorer was taken at his word were over. Having demanded that Cook provide proofs of his claim, Peary was now obliged to submit his own data to an appropriate scientific body. He chose the National Geographic Society of America, one of the sponsors of his own expedition. The three-man panel was unanimous in approving his claim to have reached the North Pole, and in the spring of 1910 Peary sailed off for a triumphant tour of the capitals and Geographical Societies of Europe. But in America seeds of doubt had been sown. The organisation that sponsored his expedition could scarcely be regarded as an impartial adjudicator on the validity of his claim. In the wake of the Cook affair, many Americans believed that Peary was getting an easy ride. He had a powerful lobby behind him, but did he really have any more evidence than his rival that *he* had reached the Pole?

When Peary sought promotion and retirement at the rank of Rear Admiral in recognition of his achievement, he was required to appear before a Congressional Subcommittee on Naval Affairs and prove that he had reached the North Pole. Here he encountered tenacious scepticism. The 'Peary Hearings' of 1911 exposed anomalies and improbabilities in his account of the journey to the Pole that were bitterly debated for the rest of his life and are a subject of controversy to this day. They ruled narrowly in his favour, but at least one of the Congressmen emerged believing Peary had something to hide.

He refused to hand over his original diary, and was unable to explain how he had accomplished the feat of travelling in a straight line over the constantly moving sea ice between Cape Columbia and the Pole – without, as he admitted, making any observations for longitude. He could not have fixed his position. How, then, could Peary have judged that he was on course?

However, the main thrust of their questioning was aimed at the daily distances Peary claimed to have travelled. When Bartlett turned back, Peary was still 130 miles short of the Pole, yet he arrived at the *Roosevelt* only two days after Bartlett, claiming to have travelled 260 miles further.

Frequently monosyllabic, Peary simply insisted that he had done it, and the Congressmen were unable to pursue the matter to a conclusion, due to their limited understanding of navigation and of Arctic conditions. One asked Peary if objects became, as he had heard, strangely magnified in the Polar regions, such that 'an ordinary hare would be the size of a good-sized animal, and that an object that might appear small here would be about the size of a mountain'. It was put to him that diminished centrifugal force at the Pole caused feeble-mindedness, to which Peary replied: 'I've never heard of the matter.' There was much bickering between the interviewers and hectoring of Peary. His wife Jo wrote:

> No one will ever know how the attack on my husband's
> veracity affected him, who had never had his word doubted in
> any thing at any time in his life. He could not believe it. And the
> personal grilling at the hands of Congress, while his scientific
> observations were examined and worked out, although it
> resulted in his complete vindication, hurt him more than all the
> hardships he endured in his sixteen years of research in the
> Arctic regions and did more toward the breaking down of his
> iron constitution than anything he experienced in his
> explorations.

Nine years later Peary was dead, of the anaemia Cook claimed to have diagnosed in 1901. He was buried at Arlington National Cemetery, Washington DC. His monument is a globe with a gold star marking the North Pole. On the plinth is the motto he inscribed on the wall of his hut at Fort Conger in January 1899: '*Inveniam viam aut faciam*' – I shall find a way or make one.

Explorers, navigators, and students of the Polar Controversy continued to argue the pros and cons of Peary's claim long after his death. Many believe that the sledging speeds he claimed are preposterous. Of the handful of expeditions that have subsequently travelled by dog sled to the Pole, none has got close to Peary's daily distances, and yet none has done it in the same way as Peary, with a fleet of supporting parties that kept the best dogs for the final dash. None of them was driven by the will of a monomaniac. Almost all of the expeditions did not make the return journey, on which Peary claimed to have made up time by following a broken trail, making two marches between sleeps and using igloos that had already been built. Some of those who have travelled near the Pole report difficult ice conditions, while others saw long flat plains that could be crossed at speed. From one year to the next, the ice is never the same.

Few believe that it is possible to navigate in a straight line across moving ice without taking observations for longitude. No satisfactory explanation has emerged from those who are convinced that he reached the Pole for the blank pages in his diary on the days that he spent there: his only entry was inserted on a loose leaf. These anomalies, the sledging speeds, and his stonewall performance at the Congressional hearings have weighed heavily against Peary, and in modern times his story attracts more doubters than believers. Among the sceptics, the arguments are about whether Peary drifted off course and then lied about the true position of his 'North Pole' camp in order to conceal his error – or if he systematically exaggerated the distances he covered.

In the pages of history books and encyclopaedias, Robert Peary is listed as the discoverer of the North Pole. In his lifetime, although the prize was tarnished, he achieved the fame that he craved. The advertisements in popular magazines of the period are an index of his celebrity. 'The underclothes that Peary wore ninety degrees north bore this label' claims the Norfolk and New Brunswick Hosiery Company. When shaving his chin in the frozen north, 'Peary realised that he had to have a brush that would last', and chose one manufactured by Rubberset of Newark. He might never have reached the Pole, readers learned, without the help of the Shredded Wheat Company.

Dr Frederick Cook never retracted his claim. By the time he returned to the United States at the end of 1910, he had begun to write *My Attainment of the Pole* and to mix self-defence with vituperative attacks on his critics. The narrative of his Polar journey begins and ends with a rabid assault on Peary:

> That I have been too charitable with those who attempted to
> steal the justly deserved honours of my achievement, I am now
> convinced; when desirable, I shall now . . . use the knife.

Reviewing Peary's career, Cook described his removal of the Cape York meteorites as 'high-handed, monumental and dishonourable theft'. He accused Peary of ignoring the suffering of the Eskimos he brought back to New York, and hinted darkly at his 'inhuman doings' amongst the people of Cape Sabine. Peary 'attempted to make a private preserve of the unclaimed North' by thwarting the work of other explorers and stealing Cook's supplies from his hut at Annoatok: 'His deliberate act was in itself – whether so designed or not – an effort to kill a brother explorer. The stains of at least a dozen other lives are on this man.'

When the Brooklyn Institute of Arts prepared to celebrate the second anniversary of Peary's attainment of the Pole, Cook marked the occasion by sending them a long letter about his former colleague. His subject was Peary's exploitation of the Eskimos, for commercial gain (in furs and ivory) and sexual gratification:

> the ship Roosevelt was used as a harem. This ship was flying the American Flag, was engaged in a mission for which the government was responsible, was equipped at public expense, its leader drawing an unearned pay as a naval officer. I charge that this ship was used as a den to satisfy a craving which leads to moral rottenness . . . Will you have our wives and daughters shake this man's unclean hands?

In a telegram to President Taft, Cook urged him not to sign the bill promoting Peary to Rear Admiral. 'Peary,' he told the President, 'is covered with the scabs of unmentionable indecency.'

For readers who had not yet made up their minds about Cook, the publication of *My Attainment of the Pole* did little to enhance his credibility. Strident and rhetorical, it added nothing to the data rejected in Copenhagen. According to one reviewer, it was no more than a 'crescendo of assertion' that he had reached the Pole. The book's frequently maniacal prose convinced some readers that Cook was mentally unbalanced and had succeeded in deluding himself.

Cook continued to press his case in a series of lectures in Europe and America. Many still found him persuasive; others came to see the famous swindler speak and to throw eggs at him. If Cook's critics believed he was merely exploiting his notoriety for the sake of financial gain, they admired his courage in including Copenhagen on his lecture itinerary.

In 1915 Cook announced the departure of a new expedition: to climb

Mount Everest. However, the British were by now at war, and Cook, born of German parents whose original name was Koch, seemed to arouse their suspicions. He was arrested in Rangoon and detained in Calcutta. Eventually they were denied permission to go to the Himalayas, and the expedition made its way to neutral Borneo to film its wildlife and indigenous peoples. Cook's luck did not improve. He entered the Texas oil business as a field geologist and was arrested in 1923 for his part in a scheme to defraud stockholders. Company lands had been falsely represented as containing oil. Cook was sentenced to fourteen years in prison, of which seven were served. In a brutal speech, the judge made it clear where he stood on the polar controversy. He regarded Cook as a career swindler:

> Cook, what have you got to say? This is one of the times when your peculiar and persuasive hypnotic personality fails you, isn't it? You have at last got to the point where you can't bunco anybody. You have come to a mountain and reached a latitude which are beyond you.

In Fort Leavenworth Penitentiary, Cook received a visit from an old shipmate. Roald Amundsen believed he owed his life to Cook's resourcefulness on the *Belgica* expedition. Of their meeting at Leavenworth and the circumstances that led to Cook's conviction, Amundsen wrote:

> Whatever Cook may have done, the Cook who did them was not the Dr Cook I knew as a young man, the soul of honour and kindliness, lion-hearted in courage. Some physical misfortune must have overtaken him to change his personality, for which he was not responsible.

A core of supporters was still defending his claim to the Pole, accusing the Peary camp of continuing their conspiracy to discredit Cook even after the Admiral's death. Before he was released from prison, oil began to flow from the lands at the centre of the legal case. Cook died on 5 August 1940, having received a Presidential pardon during his final illness. He left a voice recording, with the concluding words:

I have been humiliated and seriously hurt. But that doesn't matter any more. I'm getting old, and what does matter to me is that I want you to believe that I told the truth. I state emphatically that I, Frederick A. Cook, discovered the North Pole.

Chapter Four

BALLOONATIC

On 13 February 1895 Salomon Andrée, head of the Swedish Patent Office, founder of the Society of Swedish Inventors and famed aeronaut, stood up at a meeting of the Royal Academy of Sciences to make an announcement. Having considered the problem of making an expedition to the North Pole, he had come to the conclusion that current methods didn't work. What was needed was a technological solution:

> Has not the time come to revise this question from the very beginning and to see if we do not possibly possess any other means than the sledge for crossing these tracts? Yes, the time for doing so has certainly come, and we need not search for very long before we find a means which is, as it were, created just for such a purpose. This means is the air balloon.

Salomon August Andrée prided himself on being a man of his time. He had opinions on every topical issue from the rights of women to the living conditions of the working classes. His religion was science and rationalism. 'Mankind is only half awake,' he wrote. 'The time will come when the natural scientific method will be applied to every area.' A precocious scholar, he left his home town of Granna in Sweden at the age of fifteen in order to enrol at the State Technical University in Stockholm, and graduated four years later. Like the great Norwegian explorer Roald Amundsen, he never married and to the outside world appeared to be unattached. He published articles on the need for female emancipation but declared that as an explorer and a scientist he had to remain free of the chains of romantic attachment:

> In wedded life one has to deal with a number of factors which do not allow themselves to be arranged in accordance with some certain plan. As soon as I feel any heart leaves begin to

germinate, I am eager to uproot them.

In fact, also like Amundsen, he led a secret romantic life. Though Andrée's appetites were more subdued than those of his Norwegian colleague (known to his friends as 'The Viking'), for the last four years of his life he carried on an affair with a married woman. Andree broke off the relationship in 1897, fearing public scandal if their love was revealed, but if he was cagey about his love-life he never disguised his passion for hydrogen balloons.

He first encountered them in the USA in 1872 when he visited the World's Exposition in Philadelphia. He was immediately smitten and though he couldn't afford to pay for a test flight, he spent as much time as he could during the following months with an experienced American aeronaut, learning the ropes and gases. His first flight was a disaster: the balloon burst before it got off the ground. Although his enthusiasm was undiminished, it would take many years before he got another chance.

Andrée's ascent up the ranks of Sweden's technocracy was rather more successful. When he returned to Stockholm he secured a position as an assistant at his old university, and in 1882 was chosen to take part in a Swedish expedition to the Arctic island of Spitsbergen. Andrée conducted a series of experiments on aero-electricity, and a rather more bizarre experiment on himself. His colleagues had noticed that after several months in the darkness of the Arctic winter, their skin appeared to turn yellow. Was this a trick of the eye or had it actually changed colour? There was only one way to find out: for a month Andrée sealed himself into a shuttered house at Cape Thordsen, before emerging to confirm that prolonged absence from daylight would indeed turn human skin yellowish-green. He noted in his diary: 'Dangerous? Perhaps. But what am I worth?'

Experimenting on himself became a professional habit, and another series of tests was conducted up to 1893, when he persuaded several rich patrons to provide finance for his own balloon, the *Svea*. Over the next two years he made nine flights, spending forty hours in the air and thus becoming the most famous balloonist in Sweden. On his first ascent he took a mirror with him to observe the changes in his skin colour at different heights. On his fifth ascent he reached a height of 14,250 feet and observed that it gave him a headache.

Far more important than these observations was an idea that he had on his third flight in October 1893. Most of his contemporaries accepted that they were essentially at the mercy of the prevailing winds. Alterations of course could be made by ascending or descending, since the direction of wind currents changes with altitude, but there was no effective way to steer a balloon without fitting an engine and transforming it into an airship. However, on a journey from Stockholm to Finland in 1893 it dawned on Andrée that the drag ropes which were attached to his balloon could also be used to direct it. These ropes were supposed to stabilise a balloon's altitude. If the sun caused the balloon to heat up, the gas would expand and cause the balloon to rise. If the sun disappeared then, conversely, the gas would contract and the balloon descend. A drag rope levelled out these fluctuations – as the balloon ascended it carried more of the rope whose weight would now force the balloon down. With more rope on the ground, the balloon would now become lighter and begin to rise. Andrée noticed that the drag ropes also tended to slow down the balloon, creating an air current across its top. If this could be caught by a sail, he surmised, the balloon would then become, to some extent, steerable. Such a balloon would be a formidable tool for exploration.

He told his friends about his ambition to make a flight to the North Pole, but it wasn't until February 1895 that he felt confident enough to make public his plans. The conquest of the Pole, he declared, was essentially a technical problem which could be solved by constructing a balloon with three fundamental characteristics. It would have to be large enough to carry three people and supplies for four months, in case of a forced landing. It would have to be sufficiently gas-tight to enable it to stay in the air for thirty days. And, above all, it would have to be steerable. According to his calculations, it would take forty-three hours to get to the Pole from Spitsbergen and six days to cross the whole of the Arctic Ocean. He appealed to Swedish national pride, claiming that it was their destiny to conquer the far North:

> Are we not called upon, before other nations, as being the most suitable to execute this great task? Just as we hope and expect that the peoples of Central and Southern Europe will explore Africa, so they, too, expect us to explore this white quarter of the globe.

Andrée was undoubtedly a charismatic figure. His supporters include prominent meteorologists and scientists and the famous Swedish explorer Baron Nordenskjöld. The dynamite magnate Alfred Nobel and the industrialist Oscar Dickson were eager converts to his cause and willingly bankrolled the project. The expedition took on the appearance of a showcase for modern technology. Andrée announced that he would take a stereoscopic camera, the latest Eastman roll film and even have a dark room on board; he would use ultra-modern aluminium cutlery and cook in an oven of ingenious design which could be suspended twenty-six feet below the balloon yet ignited from the basket by means of a rope. A specially positioned mirror would enable them to see how things were cooking.

Inevitably there were sceptics and detractors. An Austrian newspaper referred to him as either 'a fool or a swindler'. When he spoke at the British Royal Geographical Society in July 1895, he faced sustained criticism from the American General Greely and the famous British explorer Admiral Markham. Both these old Arctic hands knew full well the dangers of the Arctic and Greely had lost eighteen members of his team on the infamous Lady Franklin Bay Expedition of 1882. Andrée was unabashed. When asked what he would do if his balloon came down in the sea, his reply was succinct: 'Drown.' To accompany him, Andrée recruited Nils Strindberg, a physicist and skilled amateur photographer, and Dr Nils Ekholm, a respected meteorologist. In June 1896 he finally headed north to Dane's Island, off the coast of Spitsbergen.

In Virgo Bay his team began the arduous work of constructing a sixty-foot balloon house and then inflating the *Eagle* with 170,000 cubic feet of gas. Today most modern balloons are powered by hot air, but in Andrée's time hydrogen was used. Huge boilers were filled with a mixture of sulphuric acid and iron filings, and slowly the balloon began to fill up. Tourist ships arrived in the bay to cheer and gawk. But it wasn't to be. The southerly winds he needed did not arrive, and as the months wore on the weather deteriorated. On 16 August carrier pigeons were sent home announcing that the expedition was off, and four days later he set off back to Stockholm.

Most of his supporters remained convinced that his plan would work. Alfred Nobel offered more money, and the balloon was sent back to its manufacturer in Paris to be enlarged. But now one of his team dropped out and began to make his anxieties public. Nils Ekholm had noticed that the balloon was leaking gas at a much faster rate than anticipated and he worked out that it would take much longer to cross the Arctic than Andrée had envisaged. Andrée took on board these criticisms, but he had reached the point where he could not pull out; it had become a question of honour. If Ekholm wouldn't come then he would find someone else. His choice of Knud Fraenkel as a replacement perhaps betrayed a sense of unease. Ekholm was a respected scientist and had been a colleague of Andrée on the 1882 expedition to Spitsbergen. Fraenkel's only claim to his ticket was his skill as a sportsman and his physical strength.

And so on 18 May 1897, at the age of forty-three, Andrée set off once again for Dane's Island. Much to everyone's relief the balloon house was still standing, though in need of repair. As the team began assembling and testing their equipment there were more visits from tourist ships. Photographs from those weeks show a happy crew, cleaning sledges, experimenting with cameras, inspecting the balloon – but it was obvious that Andrée was having second thoughts. When the wind changed direction on 11 July and take-off became a possibility, he became strangely diffident and left the final decision to take off to Strindberg and Fraenkel. In a letter to his fiancée, Strindberg reported:

> Andrée was serious and said nothing. We all went aboard
> again. We did not yet know what was to be done but at once he
> said to the captain: 'My comrades insist on starting, and as I
> have no fully valid reasons against it, I shall agree to it, although
> with some reluctance.'

Once the decision had been made the sailors immediately prepared for the ascent, dismantling the front of the balloon house and loading the supplies. At 1.43 p.m. Andrée and his team got into the basket. He made a short speech, formally christened his balloon the *Eagle*, called for 'three cheers for Old Sweden' and gave the order to cut the balloon free. Three minutes later it was in the air.

Things went wrong almost immediately. The balloon floated out across the bay, then suddenly dipped, touching the water. To keep her up Andrée and his crew had to throw out 207 kilos of precious ballast. As it began to ascend again, one of the shore party noticed that the drag ropes, vital to the balloon's steering system, were still on the beach.

Andrée had reluctantly agreed to install a series of quick-release screws in the middle of each rope which would enable the balloonists to abandon them should they become snagged on a rock or an iceberg. When the *Eagle* left the balloon house it had spiralled upwards, twisting the quick-release screws and causing the bottom half of the ropes to fall off. But this wasn't Andrée's only problem. When the balloon suddenly ascended the hydrogen inside expanded and escaped through a valve. The *Eagle* thus lost 792 pounds of carrying power in the first few minutes of its flight.

The next few hours were uneventful. They had a light meal and Andrée even managed to get a little rest. At midnight on 11 July the balloon entered thick fog and began to sink before coming to an absolute standstill. Eventually it started to move again but as it continued to drift westwards there were bad omens. A strange black bird circled around the basket and they passed over a patch of bloodstained ice, the residue of a bear's dinner. The balloonists made records in their diaries and roasted a Châteaubriand in their suspended oven.

They noted down their meal times, any animals they saw and the occasions when nature had to be relieved. According to Strindberg's almanac Andrée 'pissed' at the height of 600 metres before returning to his own diary. Here Andrée grew philosophical:

> It is not a little strange to be floating here above the Polar Sea. To be the first to have floated here in a balloon. How soon, I wonder, shall we have successors? Shall we be thought mad or will our example be followed? I cannot deny that all three of us are dominated by a feeling of pride. We think we can well face death, having done what we have done.

They released homing pigeons and dropped their message buoys:

> Our journey has hitherto gone well. We are now in over the ice, which is much broken up in all directions. Weather magnificent. In the best of humours.

The truth was that it was already a dreadful journey, and was about to get worse. Strindberg noted in his almanac how the basket soon began to repeatedly 'bump', 'stamp' and 'knock' against the ice. At one stage there were shocks every minute. Andrée banged his head and Strindberg began to vomit from motion sickness. As they passed through patches of freezing fog, the fabric of the balloon became encrusted in ice and grew heavier. Desperately the balloonists jettisoned ballast in order to stay airborne: out went the special North Pole buoy, an iron anchor and the drag rope chopper. But it was all in vain. At 7.22 a.m. on 14 July the balloon sank on to the ice-pack and the balloonists jumped out. They had travelled for 65½ hours and were 216 miles from the nearest land and about 480 miles from the North Pole. The *Eagle* had landed.

Back at the base camp on Dane's Island a mood of confidence prevailed. On 15 July the outside world received their first news of the expedition when a sealing captain shot one of Andrée's homing pigeons, and discovered his message:

July 13 at 12.30 p.m. Lat 82.2 W. Long 15 E, good speed towards E 10 south. All well. This is the third pigeon post.
Andrée

It was the only pigeon to return. As the months went by, and nothing more was heard, the worries began to grow. In 1898 the Swedish government distributed pamphlets to the inhabited regions of the Arctic, asking the people of Greenland, Siberia, Alaska and Iceland to keep a look out for Andrée and his balloon. The search for the *Eagle* soon became a wild goose chase.

Reports came in from all over the Arctic. He was spotted in the gold-fevered Klondike and simultaneously in the desolate wastes of Siberia, where his party was said to have been eaten by the local cannibals. Mysterious screams and gunshots heard on Spitsbergen were attributed to Andrée and his crew. He was seen as far south as San Francisco and as far north as Ivigtut in Greenland. An American spiritualist from Iowa, Ole Bracke, claimed that he saw Andrée in a vision and insisted that he would be found near the coast of Edam Land. All the reports came to nothing. They had simply vanished. Eventually, in 1902, Andrée was officially declared dead.

For thirty-three years the mystery remained unsolved. Andrée and his crew were immortalised in wax at Madame Tussaud's until their exhibit was dismantled due to an infestation of mice. In 1906 the

American Walter Wellman arrived at Virgo Bay on Dane's Island and dismantled Andrée's balloon house in order to build a hangar for his airship, the *America*. His own attempt on the Pole was even more disastrous than Andrée's, though at least he lived to tell the tale. Andrée might have joined the list of explorers who met an unknown fate had it not been for a stroke of luck.

On 5 August 1930 a Swedish scientific expedition landed at White Island en route to Franz Josef Land. Less than 200 miles to the east of Spitsbergen, the island was discovered in 1707 but was so inaccessible that it had rarely been visited. Almost all of its interior was covered by an ice cap; there were only two narrow strips of beach at either end of the island which could be landed on. The scientists took geological samples and then returned to their ship, the *Bratvaag*. The next day boats were sent out to hunt walrus, and two sailors made a remarkable discovery: Andrée's camp. They rushed back to the ship to fetch the scientists. Amid the snow and ice they found pitiful remains from the last days of the expedition: monogrammed serviettes, a Primus stove still half full of kerosene, several books and a pile of aluminium crockery. There was a boat, still lashed to a sledge, full of equipment. They found the skeleton of a polar bear, and leaning up against a rock, a pair of human legs and the remains of a body. Much of the torso was missing and the skull was nowhere to be seen, but inside the corpse's jacket they saw the letter 'A'. A diary in the pocket confirmed their suspicions that these were the mortal remains of Salomon August Andrée. In 1898 White Island had been visited by a search party looking for traces of Andrée, but they had found nothing. It was pure chance that this year the snow had melted sufficiently to reveal its secrets.

The scientists discovered Strindberg's body and gathered up as much as they could of the camp before continuing on their way to Franz Josef Land, seemingly oblivious to the fact that they had stumbled upon one of the greatest scoops of the decade. On 8 August the *Bratvaag* came across a sealing ship bound for Norway and gave the captain a letter containing news of their discovery. When the *Bratvaag* finally arrived back in the small port of Skjaervo, it was greeted by swarms of pressmen desperate to hear more; when the expedition docked at Tromsø in Norway there was a Swedish Royal Commission there to meet them.

With great ceremony the boat was unloaded and the bodies taken to Tromsø hospital to be assembled on marble slabs. Another expedition went north and returned with Fraenkel's bones and more artefacts. Andrée was elevated to the status of national hero; 75,000 people came to pay their respects as the ship carrying his remains passed Gottenburg. In Stockholm, they were accompanied by flotilla of ships and the King of Sweden made a speech on the quayside. After an elaborate funeral at St Nicholas Church the bodies were taken to the city crematorium and delivered to the flames on 9 October 1930: a final union of fire and ice.

In the following months the official investigators made some remarkable discoveries. In addition to all the equipment, they recovered two of Andrée's diaries, Strindberg's almanac and a number of his letters. Most astonishing of all, they found a number of rolls of exposed negative film sealed in metal cylinders. Thirty-three years after their sell-by date, experts began the delicate work of developing them. Amazingly they were able to process fifty prints with traces of images, twenty of which were remarkably detailed. They reveal moments literally frozen in time: the crew posing by the balloon basket, Andrée standing on a packing case surveying the wilderness, a self-timer photograph of the three men dragging a boat across the ice. What were they thinking?

Andrée's diaries provided some answers. The second diary was so badly damaged that only a few words remained on each page, but the first book, which began on 11 July and ended on 1 October, gave an amazingly detailed picture of events. In 1897 Andrée had taken the precaution of setting up a number of food caches on the north coast of Spitsbergen and Franz Josef Land in case something went wrong. When they landed on 14 July they decided to head for one of these, some 216 miles away at Cape Flora on Franz Josef Land. Confidence seemed to be high. The previous year the Norwegian explorer Fridtjof Nansen had survived eight months over-wintering on the same island after his record-breaking attempt on the Pole. But while he was a veteran of several expeditions, none of Andrée's team had any experience of the pack ice.

On 22 July they started their trek. Almost immediately Strindberg's sledge fell into the water. Andrée's diary recorded:

The travelling bad and we were extremely fatigued. Dangerous ferryings and violent listings of the sledges among the hummocks. Followed the edge of a large lead almost the whole time . . . question of lightening the load but no decision.

After four backbreaking days, a sextant observation revealed that they had travelled less than two miles. Abandoning some of their provisions and equipment, they made progress, but conditions grew worse. On 29 July he wrote:

Ate in tent. Champagne, biscuits and honey. I swept the tent with the strawcap of the champagne bottle. Grass between the stockings. Even Fraenkel complained of fatigue . . . we learn the poor man's way: to make use of everything. We also learn the art of living from one day to the next.

Fraenkel developed snow blindness, then severe diarrhoea; Andrée fell into the freezing water.

On 3 August they realised that for the last two weeks they had been fighting their way against an ice current running in the opposite direction to the course they had set. They decided to head south towards the Seven Islands, a journey which Andrée believed would take them between six and seven weeks.

As time went on they became more dependent on hunting to supplement the provisions which they dragged behind them. Andrée's diary became a bizarre Arctic recipe book. Polar bear meat was the mainstay of their diet. They found it to be so tough that it bent their aluminium forks, so they had to fashion new ones. Naturally, like all good scientists, they then took a photograph to record the evolution of their cutlery. At first they were rather particular about which parts of the animal they ate, but Andrée's diary reveals that they became increasingly innovative:

This evening on my proposal we tasted what raw meat was like. Raw bear with salt tastes like oysters and we hardly wanted to fry it. Raw brain is also very good and the bear's meat was easily eaten raw. Just as we were pitching our tent three bears came to attack us. We took up position near a hummock. Strindberg shot the old one with one ball. Fraenkel shot the other two. I fired four shots at the other cub and made hits with all but his wounds were not so serious but that he could manage to get away among the fissures and pools. We took the best bits, two thirds of the tongue, the kidneys and the brains. We also took the blood and Fraenkel was instructed to make blood-pancake (my proposal). He did this by using oatmeal and frying in butter after which it was eaten with butter and found to be quite excellent . . . the algae soup (green) was proposed by Strindberg and should be considered as a fairly important discovery for travellers in these tracts.

Throughout this early period they continued to make scientific observations. Andrée was excited to find traces of soil embedded in some glacial ice. He dissected the eyeball of an ivory gull in order to discover whether it contained some mechanism to prevent snow blindness. Their obsessive recording of bodily functions continued. In the first half of the diary Andrée noted how frequently Strindberg 'dropped'; in the second half he recorded incidences of diarrhoea amongst the team.

In spite of all their problems, their diaries give the impression of a remarkably happy group. Apart from one reference to dissent, Andrée is fulsome in his praise for their team spirit. They held frequent parties, toasting the King of Sweden with champagne and celebrating both Strindberg's fiancée's birthday and his own. Strindberg even began making notes in his almanac suggesting alterations to the balloon for the next trip.

Cheerfully or not, they were heading inexorably towards their doom. It was growing colder and almost every day they found ice on the inside of their tent. Fraenkel developed severe frostbite in his foot. The long hours hauling sledges were getting them nowhere, as the ice currents continued to thwart their progress. They realised that they were probably going to have to winter on the pack ice and began building an igloo on an ice-floe which they christened 'Home'. On 16 September they saw land for the first time: the inhospitable ice cap of White Island. They decided to remain where they were. But on the 1 October their ice-floe suddenly broke up, scattering their possessions around them. Strindberg noted in his diary that it was an 'Exciting Situation'. They would have no choice but to move ashore. Here Andrée's first diary ended:

Our large beautiful floe had been splintered into a number of little floes . . . but the floe that remained to us had a diameter of only 24 metres and one wall of the hut might be said rather to hang from the roof than to support it. This was a great alteration in our position and our prospects. The hut and the floe could not give us shelter and still we were obliged to stay there for the present at least. We were frivolous enough to lie in the hut the following night too. Perhaps it was because the day was rather tiring. Our belongings were scattered among several blocks and these were driving here and there so we had to hurry. Two bear-bodies, representing provisions for 3-4 months were lying on a separate floe and so on. Luckily the weather was beautiful so that we could work in haste. No one had lost courage; with such comrades one should be able to manage under, I may say, any circumstances.

Andrée's second diary is four pages long and so badly damaged that most of the words are indecipherable. Strindberg continued to write notes in his almanac, but the entries gradually became shorter. It appears that when they landed on shore they set up camp in the lee of a hill. They began to collect driftwood, perhaps to build a hut. Strindberg evidently died first, as his body was discovered under a pile of stones. Andrée's headless skeleton was found propped up against a rock; Fraenkel's bones were scattered around the camp. The bears had taken their revenge.

Though the diary filled in the blanks on the map of the expedition, it offered only tantalising clues in answer to the question: Why did they actually die? The obvious explanation, most enthusiastically pursued by the Swedish committee of investigation, was the effects of cold and star-vation. Their clothing was clearly inadequate: thin cotton shirts, short socks, fine jaeger britches were suitable for a skiing trip but totally inadequate in the cruel temperatures of the Arctic. They had brought with them provisions for only four months, and by October had they had run out of many staple items. Yet the diary showed that they had been relatively successful as hunters, and there were huge lumps of decaying meat discovered around the site. Though their clothing was unsuitable, investigators found unused shirts and trousers amongst the wreckage. If they were suffering in the cold, why were these extra layers not worn? And why did Andrée and Fraenkel die with an empty sleeping bag lying between them?

In the mid-thirties a new theory emerged which won particularly vigorous support from Vilhjalmur Stefansson, the famous Arctic explorer and author of the optimistically titled book *The Friendly Arctic*. When the investigators arrived on White Island they found that Andrée's primus stove was half full of kerosene. Could it be that they died, comfortable and warm in their tent, from carbon monoxide fumes? Were their tents insufficiently ventilated? This was a recurrent danger in the Arctic: Amundsen, Stefansson himself, even William Barents as far back as 1596, had all come close to death by carbon monoxide poisoning. It took almost twenty years for the mystery to be solved.

In 1947 on Disko Island in west Greenland, there was an outbreak of trichonosis amongst a group of Eskimos. This particularly unpleasant disease is caused by tiny parasitic worms found in the flesh of certain animals. Introduced into the human bloodstream, they eat away at the muscles from within. A Danish physician, Dr Adam Tryde, heard about the epidemic and noticed how closely the symptoms of the sick Eskimos resembled the notes from Andrée's diary in which he records the decline of his colleagues' health. He wondered if this could have been the cause of Andrée's death. Two years later, Adam Tryde was given permission to examine Andrée's equipment. He succeeded in scraping off fourteen tiny pieces of meat from the inside of a sleeping bag. After three months of forensic examination he found evidence of trichonosis. Without an autopsy (their bodies had been cremated) it was impossible to establish the cause of death conclusively, but today Tryde's theory is widely accepted. Ironically, Andrée had referred to the polar bear as a 'wandering butcher's shop' and 'the polar traveller's best friend'; at one stage they were eating 2.8 lb of meat every day.

A hundred years after Andrée's death, he remains Sweden's most famous explorer. In July 1997 a four-day celebration was held at his birthplace in Granna to mark the centenary of his polar flight. Aeronauts from all over Europe took part in nightly balloon galas. Intrigued by Andrée, they admire his bravery and resourcefulness. To most of them he is a tragic rather than an heroic figure, compelled by a sense of honour to set off on an expedition he feared might end in disaster. The flight of the *Eagle* marked the end of an era for ballooning. In 1900 Count Frederick Zeppelin made his first flight in a purpose-built airship; three years later the Wright brothers made the first heavier-than-air flight in the *Kitty Hawk*. Future explorers would return to the Arctic in aeroplanes and airships and make Andrée's dream of trans-polar flight a reality, but few of these expeditions evoke the same sense of wonder as the flight of the *Eagle*.

Andrée may have been a fool, even a madman – the ultimate balloonatic – but it is impossible not to be moved by his courage and a quirky naiveté in his writing. The history of the Arctic contains many disaster stories, but few of them are so well documented as the Andrée expedition. His diary is one of the most remarkable artefacts left by any Polar explorer. Amid the obsessive recording of temperatures and bodily functions, the lists and observations, there is an intimate account of a Victorian expedition's struggle for survival on the pack ice.

September 4th 1897. On a journey such as this there is developed a sense both of the great and the little. The Great nature and the little food and other details.

Chapter Five

THE LAST VIKING

Roald Amundsen did not dare tell his mother that he had decided to become an explorer. She wanted him to be a doctor, but at fifteen he happened to read Sir John Franklin's account of the disastrous journey from Point Turnagain, during which the Englishman had eaten his own shoes, and was profoundly moved:

> *Strangely enough the thing in Sir John's narrative that appealed to me most strongly was the suffering he and his men endured. A strange ambition burned within me to endure those same sufferings.*

In secret, the young Amundsen resolved to prepare for life as an explorer. Dreaming of feats of endurance at the poles of the earth he hardened his body by taking every opportunity to play football, a game he disliked, and by cross-country skiing, at which he excelled. He told his mother that his habit of sleeping with the bedroom windows wide open, even in winter, was simply a matter of his liking fresh air, and she died without knowing the reason for her teenage son's unusual behaviour. At twenty he presented himself eagerly for his period of compulsory service in the Norwegian military, believing that army discipline would be good for his soul. When he undressed for the medical examination, the elderly doctor was impressed:

> *He said to me: 'Young man, how in the world did you ever develop such a splendid set of muscles?' I explained that I had always been fond of exercise and had taken a great deal of it. So delighted was the old gentleman at his discovery . . . that he called to a group of officers in the adjoining room to come in and*

view the novelty.

After his military service Amundsen became a sailor, and was only twenty-five when he was enrolled as first mate on the *Belgica*, en route to Antarctica. He waited another six years for the opportunity to lead his own polar expedition. When it came, he achieved a remarkable feat: between 1903 and 1906, in a small fishing vessel, Amundsen completed the first navigation by ship of the notorious Northwest Passage, succeeding where his boyhood idol had perished, and where four centuries of attempts had failed.

Further exploits beckoned. Having overcome one of the historic challenges of Arctic navigation, he prepared an expedition to capture the ultimate prize. His ship was already provisioned when he heard the bad news that Cook, and then Peary, were claiming to have already reached the North Pole.

This was a blow indeed! If I was to maintain my prestige as an explorer, I must quickly achieve a sensational success of some sort. I resolved upon a coup . . .

Robert Falcon Scott was preparing a British expedition in search of the South Pole; the 'coup' Amundsen had in mind was to turn his ship towards Antarctica and surprise the world by making a race of it. After the death of Scott and four of his companions, the reaction of the British to Amundsen's famous victory was in some quarters less than generous. The late announcement of his challenge to Scott's expedition seemed ungentlemanly, if not underhand. His use of dogs was not the British way; Scott had preferred to use any other means to pull his sledges. At a dinner given in Amundsen's honour by the Royal Geographical Society of London, Lord Curzon ended his speech by proposing that three cheers be given for his dogs – many of which the Norwegian had eaten on his return from the Pole. Proud and vain, Amundsen was not a man to tolerate Lord Curzon's irony. He was enraged by what he perceived as a 'thinly veiled insult', and never set foot in England again.

In Amundsen's view, arguments about the means of surface travel were about to become irrelevant. In the year that Peary claimed the North Pole, Louis Bleriot flew a heavier-than-air machine across the English Channel; each advance in the development of the aeroplane raised new possibilities for Arctic exploration. Amundsen's youthful fantasy of suffering in pursuit of his ambitions had been realised in the Northwest Passage and the long march to the South Pole, and a new dream, of the opportunities offered to the polar explorer by the developing technology of flight, was taking its place:

> *Century after century he had worked with his primitive means,*
> *the dog – the sledge. Day after day he had exerted himself with*
> *all his craft, all his intelligence, and all his will, yet had only*
> *covered a few miles over the ice desert . . . And now, all at once,*
> *in one moment, the whole of this was to be changed . . . No*
> *rationing, no hunger or thirst – only a short flight.*

Soon after he returned from Antarctica, Amundsen enrolled on a course of flying lessons, and in 1912 was able to add to his list of distinctions a collector's item: he was awarded the first pilot's licence issued in Norway. The outbreak of war interrupted his plans to take a small biplane on an expedition into the Arctic pack ice.

When peace came, Amundsen navigated the Northeast Passage – from Norway, across the top of Siberia, to the Bering Strait. In two long voyages Amundsen had effectively circumnavigated the entire Arctic basin, drawing a circle around the largest unmapped area on the earth's surface. Peary's journey to the Pole added only a thin line of known territory to the charts. Just what the remainder of the vast blank space concealed was a matter of speculation among geographers, but many explorers of the period believed, or liked to believe, that the Arctic contained a secret: undiscovered land. Whoever made the discovery would earn a place in history as 'the last Columbus'. Amundsen was among those certain of its existence.

When he read about a new Junkers monoplane that could stay in the air for as long as twenty-seven hours, he believed he had found the best means of unravelling the mystery. He ordered one of the machines from the factory in New York and prepared to make a giant leap across the Arctic basin from Alaska, via the North Pole, to Spitsbergen, searching for land on the way. The newspapers were sceptical, but Amundsen had proved them wrong before.

The expedition was a fiasco. The Junkers developed engine trouble on the flight from the factory, made a forced landing and was written off.

Its replacement was sent by rail. On a test flight in 1923, the ski under-carriage collapsed during their first attempt to land on the ice, the plane was damaged beyond repair and the transpolar flight was abandoned before it had begun. A short time later, the courts completed his humiliation by declaring him bankrupt. The great Norwegian was un-accustomed to failure, and journalists took the opportunity to jeer at the fallen idol. He began a lecture tour of America and wrote articles for magazines on the virtues of using airships for polar exploration, but the prospect of raising money for a new expedition now seemed remote; at fifty-four, he doubted he would live long enough even to pay off his debts. 'It seemed to me,' he admitted, 'as if the future had closed solidly against me, and that my career as an explorer had come to an inglorious end.'

The lectures were a box-office failure, and at the end of the tour Amundsen retreated to a New York hotel in 'black despair'. It was not the first time in Arctic history that an explorer down on his luck received an unexpected visit from a wealthy adventurer. The stranger who intro-duced himself was Lincoln Ellsworth, the son of a Chicago coal baron and a lifelong admirer of the famous Norwegian.

> Mr Ellsworth explained that he had an independent income and a strong thirst for adventure. If I would consent to share the command of the expedition with him, so that he might enjoy the fun of flying across the Arctic Ocean, he would undertake to provide the funds.

In fact the source of funds was to be Ellsworth's elderly and irascible father, and Amundsen would have the job of talking him into it. In the meantime, over dinner in the hotel, they formulated a plan for the expe-dition and discussed what it might achieve. Ellsworth was not merely a seeker of thrills; he was a serious student of Arctic exploration who shared Amundsen's conviction that a great discovery was waiting to be made:

> It interested neither of us merely to attain the North Pole. Dr Harris, of the US Coast and Geodetic Survey, after studying tidal currents along the Arctic coast of Alaska, had formed the theory of a large body of land lying between the North Pole and North

*America. A million square miles of the Arctic there were still
unexplored; it was possible for that supposed land to be almost
continental in size.*

Ellsworth's father wavered, but was so impressed by a meeting with
Amundsen that he wrote out a cheque for $85,000. He imposed only
one condition on his 44-year-old son: 'Lincoln, if I give you this money,
will you promise never to touch tobacco again?'

Ellsworth took the money and carried on smoking. For Amundsen,
'the gloom of the past year rolled away' as preparations began for the
new expedition. To fly by airship was beyond their means, and aeroplanes fitted with skis were too fragile for landings on sea ice, as
Amundsen had learned to his cost. Their solution was to make the flight
in two Dornier-WAL seaplanes, suitable for landing on both ice and
water. Resembling a long motor boat suspended beneath a single wing,
the German machine was in fact the latest in aeroplane technology,
capable of lifting almost twice its own weight and of flying enormous distances. Twin engines were mounted above the wing, one in front of the
other (one pulled while the other pushed). Should one fail, the other was
powerful enough to lift a lightly loaded plane into the sky. Each plane
would carry three men, survival equipment including tents and sledges,
and rations for a month. For the job of flying them, Amundsen chose two
distinguished Norwegian naval pilots, Hjalmar Riiser-Larsen, and Leif
Dietrichson.

At $40,000 each, the two aircraft used virtually all Ellsworth's
money. The remaining expenses of the expedition would be met through
arrangements with newspapers, film companies and publishers, by giving lectures and by issuing – with the co-operation of the Norwegian
government – a set of commemorative postage stamps.

The Dorniers were ordered from a factory in Italy. In order to avoid
the cost of shipping them through America to a starting point in Alaska,
it was decided to begin the flight from Spitsbergen, on the European side
of the Arctic. The plan Amundsen announced to the press was to 'trek
in, as far as possible, over the unknown stretch between Spitsbergen
and the Pole in order to find out what *is* there, or what *isn't* there.' This
was as much as one of their sponsors, the Aero Club of Norway, was
prepared to sanction. Secretly, he had made an agreement with
Ellsworth that was as vague as it was risky. If conditions were favourable

they would attempt to land both Dorniers on the ice at the North Pole, transfer all the men and remaining fuel into one plane, abandon the other, and extend the flight to Alaska. The Pole was good for publicity, but it was on this second leg of the journey that they hoped to make headlines by discovering new land – 'Amundsen Land'.

As the expedition took shape and Ellsworth's excitement mounted, his father began to have second thoughts. A mysterious letter from a well-wisher urged the old man to 'investigate the circumstances' of Amundsen's proposed flight; if he did, the correspondent promised, he would never let his son go with him. James Ellsworth decided to seek first-hand advice: Robert Peary was dead, so he summoned the late Admiral's black companion to his house in order to ask his opinion about flying to the North Pole.

Matthew Henson was the only living man, other than the four Greenland Eskimos from the Peary expedition, who had been there. He told James Ellsworth what he wanted to hear – that the proposed flight was impossible: 'There is nothing at the North Pole but howling blizzards and ice piled up high like mountains.' When Henson's comments made no impression on his son he threatened to suspend his allowance and even cut off his inheritance. Eventually, he telephoned the Vice-President and tried to persuade him to cancel his passport.

But there was no turning back. The two Dorniers were shipped to Spitsbergen in mid-April, uncrated and assembled. They were known simply by their factory identification numbers, N24 and N25. Ellsworth's plane, the N24, was piloted by Dietrichson, with the mechanic Oskar Omdal sitting behind him. Amundsen's men, in the N25, were Riiser-Larsen and Karl Feucht. Amundsen and Ellsworth took the navigator's position in the nose of each aircraft. They would have to overcome unique difficulties in order to maintain their course. No maps existed. Flying over a landscape without features, there would be no points of reference and no immediate sense of altitude. Sextant observations would be impossible if the horizon were invisible behind a blur of sky and ice. Magnetism was likely to be weak, and its variations between Spitsbergen and the Pole were unknown. Yet the consequences of losing their way in so vast a wilderness could be fatal. They would have to rely on their instruments. In addition to sextants and magnetic compasses, each aircraft was fitted with a specially manufactured sun compass, designed by Amundsen: it was a clockwork device that enabled the navigator to maintain a heading in relation to the moving position of the sun.

On 21 May the seaplanes taxied on to the ice of King's Bay. Amundsen's plane was the first to take off. He felt the ice bend beneath them as they began to speed across the fjord; at 60 m.p.h. it felt to Amundsen 'like a hurricane'. Water began to surge through the buckling ice and for a moment he wondered if the load was too great – 'then, suddenly, the miracle happened'.

They rose quickly to 1200 feet. At first there seemed to be no sign of Ellsworth's plane, but soon Amundsen saw the glitter of the sun on its wing, and the N24 drew alongside. They exchanged waves from their open cockpits and turned north. An hour beyond Spitsbergen the open sea was suddenly obscured by thick fog; reflected against it, each crew saw a spectral image of their plane, surrounded by a multi-coloured double halo. It seemed to be a good omen. When the fog suddenly vanished two hours later, it revealed for the first time what Amundsen called 'the great shining plain of the notorious pack ice'. To Ellsworth, it was the realisation of a dream:

> *All my life, it seemed, I had been reading about the Arctic pack ice ... Now at last I was beholding it with my own eyes ... Ahead and to east and west as far as the eye could reach it spread, netted over with narrow cracks – the famous 'leads' about which I had read – and off toward the northwest the sun drew a gleaming trail over it. I thought I had never seen anything so beautiful.*

As they cruised at 75 m.p.h., Ellsworth reflected on the comparison with Robert Peary's twenty-year struggle to cover the 413 miles between Cape Columbia and the North Pole. From their altitude of 3000 feet, Ellsworth estimated that he could see as far as sixty or seventy miles in each direction. 'Every hour,' he calculated, 'we added to known geography more than 9000 square miles of the earth's surface.'

The hours passed and the ice fields rolled by, vast and unvarying. Gradually, their excitement was worn down. Amundsen wrote:

> *A more monotonous territory it had never been my lot to see. Not the slightest change. Had I not been engaged in making many*

*kind of observations and notes it is certain that the uniformity of
the outlook and the monotony of the engine's hum would have
sent me to sleep . . . Riiser-Larsen confessed to me later that he
had had a little snooze.*

After seven hours, Feucht told Amundsen that half the fuel had been
used, and they began to look for a landing place. They had passed the
88th parallel, but were uncertain of their longitude and therefore of their
exact position. Amundsen's intention was to land, make a series of
navigational observations, and then, in keeping with the vagueness of
his plan, 'act in the best way according to the conditions'. The N25
began a spiral descent towards a network of leads, Amundsen waving to
the other plane to follow. He was reluctant to land on the water, where
they would be at risk from the ice closing in around them and crushing
the aircraft. As they descended, they hoped to see a smooth floe, but
suddenly it was no longer a matter of choice: the rear engine cut out, and
the heavy plane began to fall short of the open water. Riiser-Larsen
brought them down in a narrow lead of slush: they veered to the left to
avoid a small iceberg, skimmed the top of another with the starboard
wing and came to rest within inches of the ice bank at the end of the
lead.

Watching from the N24, Dietrichson thought Riiser-Larsen 'must
have gone mad to pick such a hole'. But he found that his own options
were little better. As the N24 descended, Ellsworth was horrified by the
appearance of the ice in close-up:

*I have never looked down on a more terrifying place to land an
airplane . . . Great blocks of ice were upended or piled one upon
another. Pressure ridges stood up like fortress walls. The leads
that had looked so innocent from aloft proved to be gulches and
miniature canyons. In them, amid a chaos of floes and slush ice,
floated veritable bergs of old blue Arctic ice, twenty, thirty, and
even forty feet thick.*

Dietrichson landed the N24 in a small ice-free lead, and the three men
clambered out. They gazed in silence at their desolate surroundings. To
Ellsworth, they seemed to have landed in 'the kingdom of death'. A sextant observation revealed that they had drifted to the west and were – to

their disappointment – 136 miles short of the Pole. Omdal now discovered that the Dornier's rear engine was badly damaged, and the hull leaking. The plane was wrecked.

Although they believed they had come down within a mile of Amundsen's plane, they were unable to see it until they climbed on to the highest ridge. It appeared to be at least three miles away. Through his binoculars, Ellsworth could see tiny black figures walking around the aircraft, which seemed to be pitched at an alarming angle against a wall of ice.

Amundsen did not hear their shouts or see the flag they waved, and it was not until the next day that they attracted his attention. By flagging in Morse code, Amundsen informed Ellsworth's party that the N25 was undamaged – Feucht had repaired the engine. All three men from the N24 now set out across the ice, but were thwarted by a broad lead close to Amundsen's plane; he signalled to them to go back. It took them seven hours to retrace their steps over the rugged ice and waist-deep snow.

Luck was with them in the drift of the ice-pack: it was gradually reducing the distance between the two camps. On the night of 25 May the drift suddenly increased and brought Amundsen's plane within half a mile of the N24. They were now close enough to use their flags to communicate in semaphore. It was agreed that Ellsworth's party should cross the lead immediately and that all six men should concentrate their efforts on freeing the N25 from the ice that was threatening to crush it.

Amundsen watched the three men begin the short journey towards him, until they passed out of sight behind an iceberg. A short time later he heard 'a ringing shriek – a shriek which went to my marrow and made my hair stand on end. It was followed by a number of cries.' Amundsen was in no doubt that one or all of the party had fallen through the ice.

Dietrichson and Omdal had crashed through the surface in quick succession; Ellsworth, feeling the ice beneath him give way, managed to jump to safety. Crawling on his stomach across the fragile ice, Ellsworth extended his skis towards Dietrichson's groping hands – he grabbed them, and though the metal cut into his fingers, Ellsworth hauled him out. Omdal was by now crying 'I'm gone! I'm gone!', his bloodless face the only part of him visible. The current had sucked his legs under the ice and left him clinging to its broken edge by his finger-nails and teeth. Ellsworth reached him with his skis, and with

Dietrichson's help pulled him on to the surface. When they arrived at Amundsen's camp, Omdal discovered that five of his front teeth were missing.

'Five days had wrought a shocking change in Amundsen,' wrote Ellsworth. He seemed to have aged ten years. The N25 was locked in the ice. The narrow lead on which Riiser-Larsen landed the plane had closed. As far as they could see from the camp, there was neither open water, nor an ice-floe sufficiently long and flat to launch the plane. So grim had the situation seemed to Amundsen that the day after landing he had loaded a sledge in readiness to walk to the nearest point of land at Cape Columbia, more than 400 miles away. But with only a month of rations and a tiny canvas boat, he knew they had little chance of surviving the journey. Their only realistic hope of escape lay with the aircraft, and in finding a means of taking off. They would have to build a runway on the ice.

Amundsen set a deadline of 15 June: if they had not succeeded by that date they would begin to walk. It would be better than waiting for death to come to them. In the meantime, they decided to record their experiences with a movie camera.

He immediately imposed an orderly regime on the men. Rations were reduced to eight ounces per day. There were to be 'fixed hours for meals, for work and sleep, and for smoking and talking', although Ellsworth found that the Norwegians did not talk much. They threw themselves into their work. When all six men set to the task, the N25 was quickly freed and driven on to the safety of a solid floe. A petrol tank from the N24 was brought across by sledge, with some of the remaining provisions. Secure, refuelled and in working order, at least the machine was ready.

On 1 June Riiser-Larsen decided that the ice on a newly frozen lead was thick enough to attempt a take-off, and the men set to work to level the surface, using as makeshift tools their ice-anchors, hand knives, and even the camera tripod. 'How hopeless much of this work appeared to be when we started,' Amundsen wrote, 'but self-confidence and unity quickly changed the prospects.'

The eight-inch crust of ice proved to be too thin. The N25 immediately broke through, and in attempting to gather speed succeeded only in cutting a channel along the length of the runway. Before they could turn the plane around and try to rise from the stretch of water the plane had left in its wake, fog descended, and by the morning the ice had closed in again. By 5 June three further attempts had ended in failure.

'When it is darkest,' Amundsen was fond of saying, 'there is always light ahead.' The veteran explorer's quiet resolution gave the men confidence. Only Feucht, the German mechanic, was overwhelmed by their predicament. His defeatism annoyed the others, and Ellsworth admitted taking 'subtle revenge' by waiting until the German had finished his rations before ostentatiously munching his own.

> When the rest of us were down on our knees chopping at the ice, we would see Feucht leaning on his ski staff and simply staring down at the snow. It took a sharp word to bring him to his senses. To add to his misery, he developed an abscessed tooth and a swollen jaw. We came upon him one day leaning against the plane's hull as he tried to extract the tooth with a monkey wrench. The rest of us helped him.

Work now began to clear a 500-yard runway on a large ice-floe discovered by Riiser-Larsen and Dietrichson. A blanket of snow two feet deep would have to be removed. They began to shovel it to the sides, until Omdal suggested that the snow could be trampled down and left to freeze into a hard track. The many gaps in the surface were plugged with blocks of ice. By 11 June the men were close to exhaustion: 'the clang of the spades got slower, the rest intervals longer and longer, till in the end we stood quite still and stared at each other.' Amundsen estimated that they cleared more than five hundred tons of ice and snow.

On 14 June they made five attempts from the new runway, but failed to reach the take-off speed of 62 m.p.h. on a surface that was still too soft. That night, however, it froze 'fine and hard', and they prepared for a final attempt. Amundsen's deadline had arrived: if they were not successful, he told them, they would have to 'collaborate and decide what could be done'. Everything that could be spared was left on the ice, including their ski boots and parkas and half their remaining provisions.

As soon as the plane began to move along the track, Amundsen noticed the difference from the day before:

> The hasty forward glide was not to be mistaken . . . it was as though N25 understood the situation. It was as though the

whole of its energy had been gathered for one last and decisive spring . . . Now – or never.

The plane rose. The belly of the aircraft cleared a pressure ridge at the end of the runway by inches, and suddenly the ice that had held them prisoner for twenty-four days began rapidly to fall away beneath them.

Seven hours later, they saw the familiar pointed mountains of northern Spitsbergen. Feucht refused to believe they had reached safety, and shouted 'No Spitsbergen! No Spitsbergen!', but the other men knew better and began to devour their remaining rations. Ellsworth ate until he vomited. They landed in a small bay. Before long, a boat passed, out hunting for seals, and they taxied out to meet it. Amundsen had been given up for dead: the Arctic seemed to have swallowed him up, just as it had swallowed up Andrée thirty years before. At first the crew of the sealer did not recognise the dirty and bearded men in the seaplane. It was Amundsen's nose, the most famous profile in Norway, that gave them away.

Once again, Amundsen was the hero of the day. When he returned to Oslo, thousands of people and a flotilla of trawlers came out to greet him. There was a salute from a squadron of British warships and a carriage procession through the city. It was a day of mixed emotions for Ellsworth. In Spitsbergen he learned that his father had died on 2 June not knowing if his son would ever come back. Amundsen recognised that their deliverance was a matter of luck. In his diary he wrote: 'God held his hand over us.'

The published objective of the expedition, to fly over the unknown territory between Spitsbergen and the Pole, had been achieved. Soon after they landed on the ice, Amundsen had made an echo sounding (using an explosive charge, a microphone, and a stop watch) which revealed that the ocean was so deep as to discount the possibility of land existing in the area. What lay beyond the Pole, however, remained a mystery. Even before they left King's Bay, Amundsen, Ellsworth and Riiser-Larsen had resolved to return to Spitsbergen the following spring and try once more to fly the full distance to Alaska. One thing was certain: they would not use aeroplanes.

Dirigibles, or steerable airships, seemed to offer every advantage over heavier-than-air machines. They could fly greater distances and their stability in the air made them better platforms for navigational sightings and for observation. Above all, they were safer. In the event of engine failure, an airship could hover while repairs were made, but an aeroplane would have to come down and trust to luck. Amundsen had no intention of trusting it any further.

Ellsworth donated $100,000 of his inheritance, and the Aero Club of Norway set to work to raise the balance of the half a million dollars the expedition was expected to cost. Riiser-Larsen, who had taken a course in the piloting of airships in England, recommended the purchase of an ingenious prototype developed by the Italian Air Force: it was only one seventh the size of the great zeppelins, yet could fly almost as far. If necessary, it could remain in the air for a month. In a meeting with the three explorers the airship's designer and pilot, Colonel Umberto Nobile, expressed great enthusiasm for the proposed flight. Whether the Italian government would agree to sell the machine was a matter of uncertainty, but their response exceeded the hopes of the expedition planners. Mussolini had taken a personal interest in the project, and with Italian prestige in mind, was prepared to sell the N1 for a fraction of its value. It was agreed that Nobile himself would take the role of commander of the airship, and that five of his Italian crew would go with him.

It was an unlikely combination of personalities: the austere Norwegian Iceman and the dapper, emotional, religious Italian, whose constant companion – even on board his airships – was a lap dog called Titina. If there was a similarity between the two men, it was in the monumental dimensions of their egos.

When Nobile gave him a lift in his car, Amundsen began to wonder about his choice of pilot. He drove steadily while following a straight line, but accelerated inexplicably at corners:

> He would press the accelerator down to the floor, and we would take the blind curve at terrific speed. Halfway round . . . Nobile would seem to come out of his cloud of abstraction, realise the danger, and frantically seek to avert it. He would jam his brakes on with all his strength, which . . . threatened to topple us over. To prevent this, he would then start zigzagging with the front wheels.

Having narrowly survived on firm ground, Amundsen was anxious about

Matthew Henson, the former hat shop
assistant who accompanied Peary on all
his major Arctic expeditions.

Dr Frederick Cook, hero of Antarctica and conqueror of Mt McKinley. (*Below*) – Cook arriving in New York in 1909 to face Peary's accusations that his journey to the North Pole was a fraud.

Robert Edwin Peary, soon after the North Pole expedition of 1909. A study in grim determination, Peary planned this publicity photograph during his return to land.

Peary rewarded the Eskimos who helped him with plates, cups, knives and sometimes guns. Dr Cook accused him of using the women as a 'harem'.

Henson in Greenland.

A sledging party crossing
a crevasse en route to
the ice-cap during
Peary's first Greenland
expedition of 1891-2.

Like a wagon train, Peary's sledges move
supplies north to Fort Conger in readiness for
his first assault on the North Pole.

One of many ethnological photographs that Peary took of
his Eskimo lover, Allakasingwah. She bore him two sons,
one of whom lives in Greenland to this day.

Peary with three Greenland huskies. The dogs appeared with him on his lecture tours.

Breaking the trail en route to the Pole, 1909. Peary's men faced pressure ridges of sea ice up to fifty feet high.

The hydrogen balloon is made ready for Dr Salomon Andrée's attempt to fly from Spitsbergen to the North Pole.

Lincoln Ellsworth and Roald Amundsen plan the ill-fated seaplane expedition of 1925.

Andrée's *Eagle* shortly after it crash-landed on the pack ice in 1897, and (*below*) the doomed explorers with one of the polar bears whose flesh eventually poisoned them. The negatives of these photographs lay on White Island for thirty-three years.

A postcard showing the Italian crew members of the airship *Norge*. Amundsen accused the Italians of stealing the credit for the expedition.

Roald Amundsen, who accumulated more polar honours than anyone in history. His career ended in controversy and disaster.

Umberto Nobile, the Italian airship engineer who
piloted the first craft to cross the Arctic Ocean in
1926. His companion, Titina, became the first
dog to see the North Pole twice.

Captain Lundborg's crashed plane with survivors of the *Italia* disaster in 1928, and the moment of rescue as the Russian icebreaker *Krassin* reaches the 'red tent'. The *Krassin* is still afloat in the docks of St Petersburg.

Gino Watkins before the departure of the British Arctic
Air Route Expedition in 1931. On the left is Dr Vilhjalmur
Stefansson, author of *The Friendly Arctic*, and Admiral
Sir William Goodenough is on the right.

The moment of crisis during Watkins' expedition. He calls down the ventilation pipe into August Courtauld's buried tent (*top*), and moments later, Courtauld emerges for the first time in five weeks.

Atle Gresli, one of the Norwegian ex-miners who fought a covert war against German meteorologists on the Arctic island of Spitsbergen (*above*).

The road to Resolute, from the town's airstrip.
Minnie Allakariallak (*below*) was among the Inuit
who were 'relocated' at Resolute Bay in 1955.

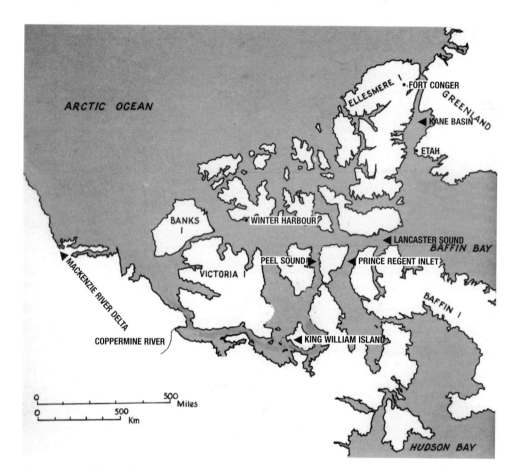

ARCTIC OCEAN

ELLESMERE I

FORT CONGER

GREENLAND

KANE BASIN

ETAH

BANKS I

WINTER HARBOUR

LANCASTER SOUND

BAFFIN BAY

MACKENZIE RIVER DELTA

PEEL SOUND

PRINCE REGENT INLET

VICTORIA I

BAFFIN I

COPPERMINE RIVER

KING WILLIAM ISLAND

500 Miles

500 Km

HUDSON BAY

CANADA'S ARCTIC ARCHIPELAGO

the Italian's performance in the air. Riiser-Larsen assured him that he knew several good pilots who were terrible drivers, and Amundsen let it pass.

The N1 was formally handed over to the Norwegians on 29 March 1926 in Rome; she was renamed *Norge* ('Norway'). By 8 April Nobile was ready to begin the 4500-mile journey to King's Bay, Spitsbergen, where a special hangar had been constructed during the winter darkness. Mussolini arrived to watch the airship's triumphal departure from Rome, his imposing physical presence somewhat diminished by a large sticking plaster covering his nose, the result of an assassination attempt the previous day. He need not have come, as bad weather over France had forced a last-minute postponement. When the *Norge* left two days later, a detour was made in order to fly over a ship carrying the Italian Premier to Tripoli.

Amundsen and Ellsworth waited at King's Bay, where twenty thousand tons of equipment had been shipped in preparation for the polar crossing. Theirs was not the only expedition flying out of Spitsbergen that spring. The American naval airman Richard Byrd and his co-pilot Floyd Bennett were preparing their large trimotor Fokker for an attempt to fly over the pack ice at a more southerly latitude, to Cape Morris Jesup, the northernmost point of Greenland.

On the morning of 7 May the Americans were amongst a small crowd gathering to watch the arrival of the *Norge*. At first the 106-metre airship was no more than a speck in the distance:

> . . . but the speck became larger, and began by degrees to take
> the shape of what was the first dirigible airship in these regions.
> The excitement . . . increased as the Norge approached and
> assumed larger and larger dimensions. Yet nothing can be
> called really large in this colossal environment . . .

The safe arrival of the airship after the long and potentially difficult flight via England, Oslo and Leningrad was cause for celebration, but the next day Amundsen was rather less buoyant. Byrd told them he had changed his mind about his flight, and would take off the following morning for the North Pole. Amundsen 'fairly bored him with his eyes', but managed to answer that it was 'all right with us'. Nobile was eager to make a race of it, and declared that the *Norge* could be ready in six hours, but

Amundsen declined. In his view Peary had already won the race, and if he coveted an ambition to be the first man to fly over the North Pole he never admitted it. Amundsen and Ellsworth maintained that their interest lay in the unknown territory between the Pole and Alaska. Nevertheless, they were now almost bound to lose out as a result of the American's change of plans. If Byrd succeeded it would diminish the value of the publicity for the *Norge* expedition. But a greater threat was that he might not come back at all. The *Norge* would then have to be used to look for him, forcing the postponement of her transpolar flight.

Byrd's trimotor Fokker took off in the early hours of 9 May. Fifteen hours later, Amundsen and Ellsworth heard the roar of its engines and rushed on to the ice to greet them. They hauled Byrd and Bennett from the plane and kissed them on both cheeks:

> We were in a great state of excitement and allowed ourselves to be carried away by our emotions . . . Nobody enquired 'Have you been to the Pole?' That went without saying, judging from the time they had been away.

The newsreel cameramen had not expected them back so soon, and were caught out. By the time the event was re-staged for their purposes, Amundsen's excitement had passed, and cinema audiences saw Byrd's welcome depicted as a series of icy handshakes.

On the morning of 11 May 1926 the crew of the *Norge* took their positions. Of the sixteen men aboard, six were Italian. The eight Norwegians included two of Amundsen's colleagues from previous expeditions: the mechanic Omdal and Oscar Wisting, who had stood at the South Pole with Amundsen in 1911. Riiser-Larsen was responsible for 'the most difficult piece of navigation a man has ever had to accomplish'. The roles of the expedition leaders during the flight were for Amundsen to observe 'as accurately as possible the region crossed', and for Ellsworth to help 'wherever he thought he could be of use'. Two red velvet chairs were provided for them. The seventeenth member of the expedition was Titina, Nobile's lap dog. He provided her with a tailor-made coat.

Nobile waited for a lull in the wind before beginning the delicate manoeuvre of leaving the hangar. At 9.55 a.m. the *Norge* rose from the ground, started her engines, and set a course for the North Pole. To the veterans of the flight of the N24 and N25, 'the feeling of safety on board the *Norge* was very much in evidence', and it increased during the airship's steady and uneventful progress northward. The wilderness of pack ice did not seem as menacing through the windows of the *Norge*: even if an engine failed, they would not have to land on it. 'Lightly and safely', they passed over the position of their lucky escape the year before.

When the Dorniers flew north they disappeared entirely from the civilised world. The *Norge*, with its greater cabin space and payload, carried sophisticated radio apparatus. At 81° 30′ N Amundsen received a telegram from a friend in Melbourne, Australia, and at 87° 30′ N the King of Norway awarded the airship's radio engineer a gold service medal. At midnight, as the *Norge* closed in on the Pole, there were further celebrations for Ellsworth's forty-sixth birthday.

At 1.30 a.m. on 12 May the cabin fell silent while Riiser-Larsen made a sextant observation of the sun. 'Now we are there,' he said, and Nobile immediately gave the order for the engines to be shut down. As the airship floated down towards the summit of the world, Ellsworth noticed the exchange of glances between Amundsen and Wisting:

I saw Oscar Wisting in the pilot house turn around and look at Amundsen. Amundsen returned his stare, and neither said a word. They were now the only men ever to reach both poles.

The flags of Norway, the United States and Italy were dropped on to the ice. An hour later, the *Norge* began the second and longer leg of her transpolar flight. The moment they left the North Pole they were travelling southward, and in the same instant entered Alaska's time zone, eleven hours behind. It was no longer Ellsworth's birthday, but the afternoon of the day before. From now on they were flying in the Arctic's uncharted zone.

The clear visibility they had enjoyed since leaving King's Bay held as far as the 85th parallel, 300 nautical miles beyond the Pole. Here Amundsen's view was suddenly obscured by fog. There were enough breaks to form an impression of the territory below them, but it was only of the monotonous continuation of the sea ice, without trace of any land.

On several occasions the fog 'rose and swamped' the airship, and Nobile feared the weight of ice forming on the ship would force them down, but they stayed aloft through a combination of skilful trimming and good fortune, for the fog could have been worse. Great alarm was caused by the sound of ice dislodged by the propellers crashing against the hull, sometimes tearing its skin and threatening to pierce the walls of the hydrogen gas chamber. The metal parts of the airship were encrusted in ice. It seemed to Nobile that the *Norge* was 'festively decorated, now that the polar crossing was on the point of being successfully achieved'.

They caught sight of the Alaskan coast at 6.45 a.m. on 13 May. Cries of relief and excitement filled the cabin. By the time they passed over it they had been in the air forty-six hours, having travelled 2000 miles across the Polar Sea. Amundsen had not seen his Promised Land, but the objective of the expedition was now fulfilled. In Ellsworth's words:

> *We could tell geographers that there is . . . no land at all*
> *between Alaska and the Pole. We had established the scientific*
> *fact that the North Polar Region is a vast, deep, ice-covered sea.*
> *The white patch on the top of the globe could now be tinted*
> *blue.*

The *Norge* eventually landed at the tiny settlement of Teller. Eskimos who watched the approach of a strange white object in the sky wondered if they were seeing the Devil.

The spectacular success of the *Norge* made headlines around the world. It appeared to provide a fitting conclusion to the illustrious career of Roald Amundsen, whose achievements at both ends of the earth now seemed to form a bridge between an heroic age of dog sledges and human endurance, and a new era of technology. However, it was not long after they completed the first transpolar flight that Amundsen and Nobile became involved in an ugly – and sometimes absurd – dispute over the credit for the expedition.

From the beginning, each man formed wildly different views of the other's status. To Amundsen, Nobile was no more than a 'hired pilot' and he likened his position to that of Captain Bob Bartlett on Peary's ship. In Italy, 'to gratify the local pride', he had given way to pressure from the Aero Club of Norway to include Nobile's name in the official title of the expedition, calling it 'The Amundsen-Ellsworth-Nobile

Transpolar Flight'. Once the *Norge* left Rome, Amundsen shortened the title at the Italian's expense.

> *I was delighted to share the national honours with my*
> *American friend. I did not intend, however, to share them with*
> *the Italians. We owed them nothing but the opportunity to buy*
> *and pay for a second-hand military dirigible.*

After the *Norge* reached Teller, he was incensed at the publicity courted and received by Nobile. The contract Nobile had signed forbade him from speaking to the newspapers, but when he found that his name did not appear in the title used in Amundsen's dispatches, he set up his own press office and presented a very different version of events. He ignored the fact that the expedition had sailed under a Norwegian flag. According to Nobile, an airship 'designed, built, and prepared in Italy and commanded by an Italian officer' had realised 'after three centuries, the dream of old Italian navigators to reach the Pacific across the north, starting from the Mediterranean'. There was faint praise for Amundsen, 'who gave his name and the benefit of his vast Arctic experience to the undertaking'.

Acting on orders from Rome, Nobile began a tour of what Mussolini called the 'Italian colonies' of America. Thousands of his compatriots turned out in the streets of Seattle to welcome him – many of them with fascist salutes.

Amundsen was disgusted by Nobile's posturing and incensed by what he saw as the theft of his expedition. He burned with hatred, and when he published his autobiography in 1927 he devoted a long chapter to insulting the Italian. The pilot's 'sole function' on the *Norge* is described as 'the management of the gas bags', and Nobile had not been very good at it. In moments of crisis, Nobile had merely wrung his hands and wept, leaving Riiser-Larsen to save the day. At the North Pole, having watched two pocket-sized flags of Norway and the United States flutter towards the ice, Nobile had produced an Italian flag of such immense proportions that 'he had difficulty in getting it out of the cabin window'. When he succeeded, it stuck to the rear of the airship and threatened to become entangled in a propeller.

There was more: Nobile had repeatedly warned the entire party to bring only a minimum of luggage, but when they reached Alaska he emerged in a 'resplendent dress uniform' of the Italian Air Force. Throughout Amundsen's 'inside story' of the flight of the *Norge*, Nobile is characterised as a man of great personal vanity, unashamed cowardice and sly ambition. The Italian's contention that he had made his own plans to fly in the Arctic many months before the Norwegians approached him was preposterous: Nobile could not even keep his footing on the ice of King's Bay. He was no more than a 'strutting dreamer' whose vanity had been manipulated by his government's propaganda machine.

> *It is merely amusing to suppose that men of this semi-tropical race, who had not the most rudimentary idea of how to take care of themselves in a cold country, could ever have conceived the notion of undertaking an expedition which required as its most elementary qualification an ability to survive on the ice in an emergency.*

My Life as an Explorer is a strange and bitter book. Its publication embarrassed Amundsen's supporters, and although it wounded Nobile it caused almost as much damage to the Norwegian's reputation. In time, Nobile answered some of the specific charges made against his conduct on the flight of the *Norge*, and he is recognised by history as the man who designed, built and piloted the first aircraft to cross the Arctic basin. As for Amundsen, he could see no irony in the fact that the successful operation of the airship had reduced his role as explorer to merely looking out of a window.

The new heroes of the Arctic were the pilots of flying machines, and Umberto Nobile, even before he left Alaska, had made plans for a new expedition.

Chapter Six

ONE MAN AND HIS DOG

'Perhaps it would be better not to tempt fate a second time,' warned Mussolini when Nobile told him that he was intending to return to the Arctic. His Air Minister was even less enthusiastic. Italo Balbo, fascist thug and acclaimed pilot, saw Nobile as a rival and airships as an anachronism. He hoped to win glory for himself and Italy by staging long-distance formation flights. Balbo refused to lend Nobile any flying boats for the expedition which he insisted should be funded by private sources.

Nobile was undeterred. After the *Norge* expedition Amundsen announced that his exploring days were over, but Nobile had been bitten by the Arctic bug. He first conceived of a return flight as a joint expedition with Riiser-Larsen a few days after the *Norge* landed in Alaska, but as the controversy developed Riiser-Larsen took Amundsen's side and so nothing came of it. In 1927 Nobile was dispatched to Japan to organise the hand-over of an Italian airship; when he came back to Italy he began looking for money in earnest. He was quickly able to raise sufficient private sponsorship from supporters in Milan to make the project viable. He would return to Spitsbergen and make a number of flights to the unexplored islands of the eastern Arctic and a second flight to the North Pole itself which would include an attempt to land a party of men on the ice to make scientific observations. If everything came off according to plan he would be firmly placed on the map as a great explorer and put an end to Amundsen's carping.

In the great tradition of polar patriotism his new airship was christened the *Italia*. All of the crew was Italian and only two foreigners were invited along: the Swedish meteorologist Finn [sic] Malmgren and Franz Behounek, a cheerful and rotund Czech scientist. To make up for his lack of experience on the ice, Nobile read up on Peary and Nansen and toured Europe, visiting leading explorers and Arctic experts. He designed special suits and survival equipment, and even came up with his own recipe for pemmican, the ubiquitous dried food of the polar explorer, which was concocted to appeal to the Italian palate. Each man would carry his own personal survival kit, which included a compass and a veil, in case they were forced to land in the Mackenzie Delta which was notorious for mosquitoes. An Italian naval ship, the *Città di Milano*, was assigned to the expedition as a support vessel.

At the end of March Nobile's crew had an audience with Pope Pius XI, who was something of a polar buff and keenly interested in their project. He presented them with a large wooden cross which they were enjoined to drop on to the North Pole 'to consecrate the summit of the world'. He added with a smile: 'And like all crosses, this one will be hard to bear.'

His prophecy came true when the *Italia* left Milan on 14 April 1928. Their journey northwards was plagued by poor weather and bad luck. When they made a stop at Stolp in northern Germany they discovered that two fins were broken and that all three propellers had been damaged by hailstones. In one of the few more cheerful moments, a message was dropped from the airship into the waiting hands of Malmgren's mother in her garden in Stockholm.

Nobile had made plans for five different flights which would be scheduled according to the best weather opportunities. His most ambitious journey would take him all the way across the Arctic to the Mackenzie Delta in Canada, but he also intended to make a series of journeys to the eastern Arctic. Unfortunately his bad luck continued. When he took off on his first flight on the 11 May, Nobile was hoping to make a 2100-mile journey to Severnaya Zemlya, but eight hours later the *Italia* limped back with a broken rudder and a snowstorm in cold pursuit.

At King's Bay his problems continued. The airship was moored in the same roofless hangar which had been specially built for the *Norge* in 1926. As the weather worsened, snow began to accumulate on the top of the airship – at one stage over one tonne per hour was falling on to its delicate skin. Nobile had no alternative but to send up gangs of workmen equipped with brooms on to the top of the airship to brush the snow off. Suddenly, though, the weather changed and Nobile set off again. This flight was much more successful and though they were not able to reach Severnaya Zemlya Nobile returned to King's Bay flushed with confidence. He had made an epic 69-hour flight to a region which was virtually unexplored; now he was ready to make another flight to the Pole itself.

Nobile estimated that it would take thirty-six hours to make the return trip but took along plenty of survival equipment in case anything should go wrong. After the Norwegian weather station at Tromsø had given him the go-ahead, at 4.28 a.m. on 23 May the *Italia* slowly rose into the air and headed north. For Nobile, the five other veterans of the *Norge* and Titina the dog, this would be a unique opportunity to become the first people to see the North Pole twice.

At first things went relatively well. Once they had passed the northern tip of Greenland they were encouraged on their way by a strong tailwind. At 12.20 that evening they slowed down, made a series of navigational checks and then Nobile announced that they had arrived at the Pole. With the jaunty tones of the national anthem blaring out from the gramophone, Nobile was cheered by the crew and toasted with home-made egg-nog. He had done it, and without the assistance of any Norwegian explorers. Radio messages were dispatched to Mussolini and the King and yet more Italian flags were dropped on to the ice along with the Papal cross.

Nobile now considered what to do next. The prevailing wind made it easier to fly eastwards towards Alaska but Malmgren, the meteorologist, predicted that it was just about to change so they headed back towards Spitsbergen. It was slow going: Nobile kept the ship very low, hoping to avoid banks of fog, but visibility was poor and the head-wind reduced their speed to 28 m.p.h. Ice started to form on the propellers and fly back into the ship, ripping its delicate outer skin. To make matters worse, at one point Trojani, the engineer, accidentally locked the elevators into a nose-down position and the *Italia* began hurtling down towards the ice. Just in time, Nobile managed to have the engines turned off and airship levelled off barely 250 feet from the ground. Nobile spent his time rushing between the navigation table, the radio room and the deck. He caught sight of a photograph of his daughter Maria which he had pinned up on a wall: 'Maria's eyes looked back at me. I was struck by the sadness of their expression. They seemed to be misted with tears.'

After they had navigated for hours by dead reckoning, the fog started to thin and they ascended to take a navigational sighting. They discovered that they were nearly 180 miles north-east of King's Bay, about five hours away from home. Then suddenly their instruments began to show that the airship was descending again. To double-check, Nobile dropped glass balls containing red dye out of the airship: by measuring how long it took for them to hit the ice he was able to calculate the ship's height. They confirmed his worst fears. It was the same problem which had brought Andrée's balloon down: ice had formed all over the envelope of the airship and increased its weight dramatically. Nobile was forced into desperate measures. The ice anchor was thrown overboard but the *Italia* continued to fall. Nobile tried turning on all the engines at full power but the descent continued. Then, realising that it was inevitable that they would crash, he ordered all the engines to be turned off and for everyone to stand at their posts. The cabin hurtled into the ice and filled up with snow. Several dye balls smashed open, staining the snow red. Nobile felt his limbs snap and a heavy object hit him on the head: 'Instinctively I shut my eyes, and with perfect lucidity and coolness formulated the thought: "It's all over!"'

Nine men were disgorged on to the pack ice. Nobile had two broken limbs and a head wound, Malmgren had dislocated his shoulder, Ceccioni had fractured his leg. Pomella, the mechanic, was found sitting on a hummock of ice with one of his shoes missing. At first they thought he was in shock, but he was dead. Malmgren turned to Nobile, thanked him for allowing him to come on the expedition and with a desperate look announced: ' I go under the water.' Nobile persuaded Malmgren not to do anything so drastic but he too held out little hope. Only Titina the dog was happy, rejoicing in her new-found freedom: 'I called her to me, but she refused to understand and continued to frisk about, wagging her tail and sniffing the air.' The *Italia*, now suddenly lighter after losing the cabin, floated off into the fog with six men on board. It was never seen again.

After a couple of hours the survivors began to look around the ice-floe on which they had been deposited. They quickly found a tin of pemmican, a signal gun and a revolver. By the end of the first day that had recovered about seventy kilos of provisions which they calculated would last them for twenty-five days if they rationed themselves to a meagre 300 grams a day. They had a single two-man tent for nine people and one sleeping bag which was cut open and shared between the two men who were most seriously injured, Nobile and Ceccioni. They did have one real stroke of luck though, recovering their emergency radio set. Immediately Biagi began transmitting SOS signals every two hours. But no one responded and their morale dropped even further. Only Malmgren had ever set foot on the pack ice before and his despair was only too clear. On the second night, Ceccioni kept everyone awake crying his eyes out.

They found a set of navigational instruments and took a sun shot: they were still approximately 180 miles from King's Bay, between twenty-five and twenty-six degrees of longitude. At night they were able to tune their receiver to the San Paolo radio station 3200 miles away in Rome, but it was a frustrating experience. They could hear newscasters reporting the disappearance of the *Italia* but it was obvious that no one had heard their SOS. To make matters worse, it appeared that the rescue operation which was getting under way was concentrating on the wrong area, many miles west of their actual position.

The crash had ironically coincided with a celebration banquet in Oslo to commemorate Hubert Wilkins' successful flight across the Arctic basin. Many of the leading Norwegian explorers were there, including Sverdrup, Riiser-Larsen and Amundsen; when they heard about the *Italia* a rescue committee was hastily convened. They were all optimistic that the crew were probably still alive but worried that there was a massive area to be searched and that there were too few long-range planes available. Riiser-Larsen offered to add extra fuel tanks to his biplane and the Swedish government agreed to send up seven aircraft and seven support ships, but they all knew that none of these would be as effective as the Italian flying boats that Nobile had initially requested.

In spite of the harsh criticism of Nobile which had just appeared in his autobiography, Amundsen quickly agreed to take part in the rescue. When he was interviewed by an Italian journalist, he was magnanimous:

Anything which has disturbed my relations with General Nobile has been forgotten for some time. Ah! If you only knew how splendid it is up there! That's where I want to die; and I wish only that death will come to me chivalrously, will overtake me in the fulfilment of a high mission, quickly without suffering.

Nobile and his men didn't share Amundsen's love for the Arctic nor his confidence that everything would soon be resolved. They had discovered that the ice-floe on which they were camped was drifting eastwards, taking them further away from Spitsbergen, and they were worried that soon their radio's batteries would run out. Their only bit of good fortune came when Malmgren spotted bear close to their camp. He crept into the tent and loaded the revolver; others grabbed knives, axes and whatever pieces of wood they could find. Nobile clutched Titina tightly in case she should bark and give the game away. In spite of his dislocated shoulder, Malmgren downed the bear with his first shot. Inside its stomach they found the partially decomposed remains of one of the *Italia*'s navigation books which the hapless bear had recently dined on.

Now they had almost 200 kilos of fresh meat, enough to last them for at least a month, but with no sign of any imminent rescue two officers came to Nobile proposing that they should attempt to walk to land. Nobile tried to put them off, but they were adamant. At one stage it looked as if most of the men wanted to go with them, but eventually three men set off – Mariano and Zappi, and the Swedish meteorologist, Malmgren. They left with a knife, fifty-five kilos of provisions and letters home from the remaining men. Malmgren estimated that it would take them about sixteen days to get to land but he hadn't recovered his good humour: 'Both parties will die,' he said.

Nobile now decided to risk increasing the number of radio transmissions, sending out the message in both Italian and English: 'SOS. *Italia*. Nobile. On the ice near Foyn Island, north-east Spitsbergen . . . impossible to move, lacking sledges and having two men injured. Dirigible lost in another locality. Reply via IDO 32.' No one replied. Then on 6 June, as Biagi bent over the radio to take down notes on the nightly news bulletin from the San Paolo station in Rome, he heard some astonishing news: 'The Soviet embassy has informed the Italian government that an SOS from the *Italia* has been picked up by a young Soviet farmer.'

It was a Russian radio ham, going by the rather more Germanic name of Nicholas Schmidt, who had picked up their transmission over 1400 miles away in a small village near Archangel. The next day they heard that the *Città di Milano* too had heard their transmission and had their correct co-ordinates. They were asked to prepare smoke signals and told that aeroplanes would soon be on their way. Nobile was jubilant. That night they celebrated with an extra ration of five pieces of sugar, ten malted milk tablets and two ounces of chocolate each.

By the middle of June a flotilla of seaplanes from Norway, Sweden, Finland and France was converging on the area in an unprecedented international rescue attempt. Nobile's supporters in Milan finally raised the money to send up two Italian seaplanes to join the search. Amundsen had turned to his old friend Ellsworth to help him buy another Dornier-WAL, but before their negotiations were concluded the French government offered to lend him one of their planes. Its crew of four was lead by René Guillbaud but Amundsen also took with him Leif Dietrichson, the veteran pilot of his 1925 expedition.

But the most significant addition to the international relief effort was a Russian ice-breaker, the *Krassin*. On 20 June it sailed from Leningrad for Bergen in Norway. The biggest ice-breaker in the world, its engines could generate 10,500 horsepower and at full speed it burnt six tons of coal per hour. The ship's company included Davide Guidici, an Italian journalist from the *Corriere della Sera*. Fortunately for him, he was able to talk to most of the crew in English but the Russian captain only knew one phrase which he repeated every time he met a foreigner: 'The *Krassin* is a very strong ship.' It needed to be.

Things were getting worse for the men on the ice. They had to move their first camp when the ice-floe which they were camped on started to break up under their feet. Another bear paid them a visit and started to dig up Pomella's grave; Trojani got off a couple of shots but this time the bear managed to escape. Then suddenly, on 17 June, they saw their first plane: it was the Norwegian Riiser-Larsen in a Brandenburg flying boat. They rushed to light smoke signals as they watched him getting closer and closer. But when it seemed to be but a few miles away, the plane abruptly turned round and disappeared.

They dyed the tent red in order to make it more visible. Nobile ordered his men to hold up broken pieces of mirror and tin to act as reflectors the next time a plane came around. He himself was now suffering from snow blindness and had constructed a pair of sunglasses from the cellophane packaging of a chocolate bar. They were a motley bunch who stood on the ice waiting to be rescued.

On 20 June one of the Italian pilots, Maddalena, set off from Spitsbergen on his second flight north. Nobile had been in contact with the *Città di Milano* and had asked for the flying boats to be fitted with radio sets so that once they came into view they could be guided to the red tent. According to plan, when Maddalena's huge Savoia Marchetti appeared on the horizon Nobile began giving him directions. It grew closer and closer and closer and then missed the camp. Half an hour later he returned and this time succeeded in dropping emergency parcels to the men below. Now they had two more sleeping bags, six pairs of new shoes, spare batteries and, most important of all, renewed hope.

Two days later they heard news that the Swedes were considering making a landing on the ice and wanted Nobile's men to mark out a suitable ice-floe. On 23 June the Swedes arrived. Leaving his engine running, Lieutenant Lundborg went to greet Nobile and his dishevelled comrades:

> In spite of his long beard and whiskers I immediately recognised the general. He was bare-headed. He wore a grey sweater and light grey knickers, one foot in a civilian summer shoe and on the other a stocking and a reindeer-skin slipper.

Nobile had drawn up a priority list for any evacuation. Number one was Ceccioni who had broken a leg, number two was the Czech Behounek because he was 'heavily built and clumsy on the ice'; Nobile himself was number four. Lundborg had different ideas. He had been ordered to bring back Nobile to co-ordinate the rescue operation. The general was reluctant to leave his men but eventually he agreed when Lundborg promised that he would come back immediately to pick up Ceccioni.

He was carried across the ice and painfully lifted into the plane. Titina had got there first. An hour later they disembarked at the improvised Swedish base on Rhyss Island, their first steps on dry land in over a month. The next day he flew on to the *Città di Milano* in Virgo Bay where he was met by cheering sailors. Gradually though, the atmosphere changed. The world's press were besieging the ship for news and Nobile's enemies in Rome had begun to plant critical stories. Years later, Nobile heard that when Balbo was notified of the disaster his response had been brutal: 'Serves him right.' Rumours spread that he had injured his leg running across the ice to Lundborg's plane, so eager was he to leave. The French newspaper *Le Matin* openly called him a coward. Captain Romagna came to his cabin with a warning: 'People might criticise you for coming first, General. It would be as well to give some explanations.' But no one took any notice when Nobile protested that he had been ordered to leave. Riiser-Larsen, the Norwegian pilot, later wrote that one of the Italians on board had even suggested that Nobile should shoot himself rather than live without honour. He himself was sure that Nobile was telling the truth: 'It was a disservice that had been rendered Nobile. The world at large turned against him . . . he however had been coaxed out on false premises.'

To add to Nobile's anguish, he heard that Amundsen had gone missing and that Lundborg's second flight to the red tent had gone terribly wrong. His plane overturned on landing and now the Swedish pilot was added to the list of the men stranded on the ice. On orders from Rome, Captain Romagna excluded Nobile from the remainder of the operation and he was left to languish in his cabin. When Riiser-Larsen visited him it was a rare moment of release:

> I found myself in the giant's arms. I flung mine around his neck.
> I could find no words to express what I felt. My eyes filled with
> tears . . . I wanted to express my gratitude for the chivalrous
> gesture with which Amundsen and he had wiped out those
> miserable squabbles of the past. But I was silent, I could not
> speak.

After twelve days at the red tent, Lundborg was rescued by another Swedish pilot, but they were reluctant to risk any further landings on the ice. All eyes turned to the *Krassin*. Its fuel was running out, one propeller had lost a blade and its steering system was damaged. Could it reach the men in time? On 10 July the *Krassin* sent out their own plane to look for the red tent. It was forced to make an emergency landing but the pilot was able to radio some remarkable news back to the ship. He had seen three men standing on the ice about fifteen miles away.

On the morning of 12 July two figures were spotted from the deck. They were Mariano and Zappi, the Italian officers who had set off on foot from the camp over a month before. But where was the third man, Malmgren? Mariano was suffering from malnutrition and gangrene but Zappi was surprisingly hearty and was able to climb aboard under his own steam. He told his saviours that Malmgren had died a month ago. He didn't understand why the pilot had reported seeing three men – maybe he had been confused by an old pair of trousers which they had laid out on the ice. Their story developed into one of the more bizarre elements of the 'Italia tragedy'. When a Russian doctor did a stool analysis on Zappi, he concluded that the brave captain had eaten two days before, not twelve, as he claimed. Zappi's list of clothes was equally mysterious: three pairs of trousers, two pairs of fur-lined boots, a knitted vest, a fur vest and a linen coat with a cap. He reported that at one stage Mariano had whispered to him: 'Zappi, when I die, you must hold out. Begin to suck my blood, then eat my brain. Try to make your stomach accept it.' As if their story wasn't sensational enough, this prompted rumours of cannibalism: had the two Italians eaten the Swede? Nobile himself regarded this idea as preposterous, though he never forgave Mariano and Zappi for leaving the other men on the ice:

> To leave Malmgren was neither cowardice nor heroism: rather it
> was a bitter necessity. In an icy wilderness, where the instinct of
> self-preservation takes the upper hand, the laws of the civilised
> world no longer apply. In similar circumstances there are no
> other laws except those of Nature, just as there are no judges
> except God and a man's own conscience.

The *Krassin* steamed on until finally, at 8.15 p.m. on 12 July, the men at the red tent saw the ship approaching. The ice-floe on which they had been living for the last month was beginning to break up. Biagi hastily tapped out a final message announcing their rescue and concluding with a Latin flourish: 'Long live Italy! Long live the King! Long live Mussolini.'

On board the *Krassin*, the men were given telegrams from well-wishers and loved ones whilst Biagi received a court summons from the authorities in Rome for non-payment of his dog licence. 'Send them up here to collect it!' he barked. The Russians turned back for Spitsbergen. There were emotional scenes when Nobile was reunited with his crew, but he was still desperate for the search to continue for the six men who had been on board the *Italia*. The *Krassin*, however, needed urgent repairs and headed back to Norway. It returned to the Arctic in September, but nothing more was found of the *Italia* and bad weather cut the voyage short.

There was still no sign of Amundsen. At first no one was too worried – after all, he had always come back from the brink of disaster before. As the weeks went by, worries grew. Riiser-Larsen was diverted from the *Italia* rescue to search for his former mentor but he found nothing. Then,

on 31 August, part of one of the seaplane's floats was discovered floating in the sea near Tromsø. Later a fuel tank was also washed up but
Amundsen's body and those of his crew have never been found. The
great polar hero was gone forever.

Nobile described his time on the ship as 'one of the worst periods of
my life, thirty-two days of indescribable torment', but worse was to
come. When the *Città di Milano* steamed into Narvik in northern
Norway, the men were immediately directed along a specially constructed walkway into a waiting train. There was such ill feeling towards
them, because of Amundsen's disappearance, that no one wanted the
Italians even to set foot on Norwegian soil. On the train Nobile read a
selection of newspapers which repeated the accusations of cowardice.
When it stopped in Sweden, the crowds were more sympathetic:

> *A little fair-haired, blue-eyed girl came towards me, smiling*
> *sweetly, to offer me a bunch of flowers. Choked with emotion I*
> *thanked her, stammering. After all, there were still pure and*
> *gentle spirits among mankind. Not all were beasts of prey.*

Going through Germany the train was jeered and heckled, but when they
arrived in Rome 200,000 people came out to greet them. In spite of the
efforts of the fascist newspapers to discredit Nobile, he was given a
hero's welcome. The government was clearly embarrassed by the whole
affair and was intent on pinning the blame on Nobile. One fascist newspaper even suggested that Nobile should be court-martialled and then
shot. He went to see Mussolini to try to tell his side of the story, but *Il
Duce* didn't want to hear. Nobile was locked out of his office and followed by the secret police. Balbo continued to spread hostile rumours:
at one stage he planted a press story demanding that Nobile's leg should
be X-rayed in order to ascertain whether he had broken his leg during
the crash or, as Balbo insinuated, if it happened when Nobile was running towards Lundborg's plane, desperate to get off the ice.

The official commission set up to look into the accident was a travesty
of justice. All the evidence was taken in private and Nobile was never told
that his conduct was under investigation. Their findings were unequivo-
cal: 'The unanimous conclusion of the commission is that the loss of the
airship was caused by an incorrect manoeuvre and the responsibility lies
in the commander.' Mariano and Zappi were praised for their bravery, but

Nobile was condemned for leaving the red tent: 'This act has no plausible justification, and it can only be explained, but not justified, by the low physical and moral condition in which he found himself.'

Nobile refused to go quietly. Instead of retiring he made a very public resignation. Though in many countries the findings of the enquiry were taken at face value, the Swedes and the Russians never lost their faith in Nobile. He was awarded the prestigious Andrée medal by Sweden and in 1931 he was invited to accompany Samoilivitch, the commander of the *Krassin*, on another scientific expedition to the Arctic. He left Italy to take charge of Russia's airship-building programme and lived there until 1936 before he left for the United States. Nobile's enemy Italo Balbo did win fame and glory by staging epic Italian Air Force formation flights, but in the early forties he was accidentally shot down by Italian guns in North Africa. After years of exile in the United States and later Spain, Nobile returned to Italy at the end of the war. A new impartial enquiry was staged into the flight of the *Italia* and Nobile's reputation was restored. He died at the age of ninety-three, two months after he took part in celebrations to mark the fiftieth anniversary of the *Italia* expedition.

With his tiny dog and large ego, Nobile was one of the more unlikely Icemen but he did have a genuine fascination with the Arctic which lasted until his death. Many other explorers endured even greater privations, but no one was treated so shabbily as Nobile on his return to Italy in 1928. Both the *Norge* and the *Italia* made incredible journeys, and with today's widespread acceptance that Byrd's flight was a fraud, Nobile could claim to be the first man to have flown to the North Pole. He was a slight man, he had been rejected from the Italian Army twice because of poor health, but his strength of character was enormous. His daughter Maria remembers how it surprised even himself:

When he would look back on those days, and when he would remember all the effort it took, all the energy, all the physical strength he needed during those flights, he was quite amazed. Almost as if it was another person, he would say.

Chapter Seven

AN ENGLISHMAN ABROAD

Gino Watkins did not look like an explorer. One of Augustine Courtauld's friends said he looked like 'a pansy'. Posing for a photograph taken in the summer of 1930 in front of the ship hired for his latest expedition to the Arctic, he is dressed as if for the French Riviera in a loose pale suit and cane. Dapper, slight, blond, fond of dance halls and sports cars, he was ostentatiously frivolous in his social life, and deadly serious about his chosen career. If he raised a few eyebrows at the Royal Geographical Society, so much the better.

He was only twenty-three and had not yet finished his degree at Cambridge. The newspapers, however, were already calling him an Arctic 'veteran'. At nineteen, having failed to find a place on a university expedition, he organised his own, to Edge Island, Spitsbergen. Two years later he was exploring the unmapped interior of Labrador. It was during this adventure that a brilliant idea occurred to him – he wanted to lead an expedition to Greenland, and had thought of a good reason for one to be sent. In 1929 he wrote to the Royal Geographical Society:

> I am anxious to study the practicability of an Air Mail Route
> from England to the Pacific coast of America, via Iceland,
> Greenland, Baffin Land, Hudson Bay and Edmonton. The
> amount of time which would be saved by using this route
> would be very great indeed, and it has the great
> recommendation of relative safety since there are few long sea
> crossings to be made . . . The part of this route which is least
> known at present is the East Coast and central ice plateau of

Greenland. The East Coast at about the point which seems most
suitably placed for the crossing is almost entirely unmapped,
and very little is known of the meteorological conditions on the
ice cap.

Nine times the size of Great Britain, Greenland is all but buried under a vast dome of solid ice that in 1930 was thought to rise – though nobody knew for certain – to a height of over 9000 feet. Towards its outer rim, where the dome slopes away, black mountain peaks penetrate the ice, and between them giant glaciers slide imperceptibly towards the sea. A single flight over Greenland would prove nothing as far as the air route was concerned. Information about average flying conditions was needed, and for this purpose Watkins proposed to maintain for one year a meteorological station high up on the plateau itself. How hard the wind blew there, and how low the temperatures fell, nobody knew.

In order to help future pilots find their way, the expedition would pro-duce the first accurate map of the section of Greenland's east coast that lay on the proposed route. For the first time in the Arctic aerial photography would be used to assist the survey. Two Gypsy Moth biplanes, transported in crates and fitted with both floats and skis, would also re-supply the meteorological station, attempt a return flight from the expedition base to Winnipeg, and finally return to England along the eastern section of the route via Iceland and the Faroe Islands.

Watkins planned a series of long journeys across the ice cap to deter-mine its altitude. These would be undertaken by dog sledge, without Eskimo tuition or assistance. Watkins intended to prove that dog-driving was a skill that could be quickly mastered by men who had never seen a husky or held a whip. He was equally determined that the expedition should learn to hunt and to support itself, for at least part of the time, on the flesh of seals, bears and other Arctic game. Like many polar travel-lers of the period, Watkins was influenced – and enlightened – by a book published in 1921 by the Icelandic explorer Vilhjalmur Stefansson. *The Friendly Arctic* is an account of his long journeys in the north; it is also an essay on survival. Stefansson did not recognise the frigid wilderness described by explorers of the Franklin era. Stefansson's Arctic was a land rich in game, where a travelling party could support itself by hunt-ing for an indefinite period. Practical advice was included, and Watkins intended to follow it.

The proposal impressed the Royal Geographical Society, and some money was made available to Watkins; the Air Ministry, the Admiralty and the War Office contributed men and equipment. Many companies provided supplies free of charge, but Watkins was left a long way short of the cash needed to purchase aeroplanes and hire a ship. He seriously considered an offer from a film company to join the expedition and shoot part of a romantic drama in Greenland. In return for the explorers' assistance on location, generous financial support would be given to the expedition. Thrilling scenes were conceived featuring emergencies in blizzards and crevasses – before Watkins decided that the scheme was ridiculous. The expedition would never have sailed for Greenland had it not been for the discreet financial support of the Courtauld family.

Augustine Courtauld had been at Cambridge at the same time as Watkins and had twice gone to the Arctic with university expeditions. Although – like everybody else – he had heard of the remarkable Watkins, they had never met. Courtauld was greatly interested in the 'British Arctic Air Route Expedition', and asked Watkins to visit the family estate (he arrived in the middle of a grouse shoot). Before long Courtauld was appointed treasurer to the expedition committee, and went to work on his uncles and aunts.

Watkins concentrated on practical details. He read widely, sought the best advice, then developed his own designs for specialist equipment and a new recipe for sledging rations. Here Watkins believed he had found the solution to an old problem – how to combine lightness with a ration of high calorific value that would sustain men working hard in bitter temperatures. It was greatly to increase the proportion of fat. Each day, the men would eat half a pound of margarine in a total ration of thirty-five and a half ounces. A professor at the Lister Institute agreed that the theory was sound, but wondered if in practice it might be asking too much of the human digestive system. There was only one way to find out: for a week of the London winter Watkins did his best to recreate Arctic conditions, sleeping without pyjamas by an open window and skating on the Hammersmith rink before a breakfast of porridge and margarine. When he was invited to dinner parties, the immaculate Watkins arrived carrying his food in a brown paper bag. The 'week of horror' left him feeling rather unwell, but he was convinced that his digestion would be more grateful for the ration on the long and arduous journeys to come.

In choosing his team, Watkins thought it wise not to bring anyone more experienced than himself. 'I prefer,' he said, 'that all . . . should have gained their knowledge with me, since in that case I always know the exact amount of experience possessed by each member of any sledging party. If anything goes wrong . . . I can judge more easily what the leader of the party will do in an emergency.' According to his friend J. M. Scott, 'he chose men chiefly because he liked and understood them and thought them sufficiently open-minded to prove adaptable to anything'. The average age of the fourteen members of the expedition party was just twenty-five. Only three had been to the Arctic before, and no fewer than ten were Cambridge men. Alfred Stephenson, the chief surveyor, had finished his final examinations a few weeks earlier.

Watkins was to win many admirers for his style of leadership. There were to be no formalities. All would share equally in the physical work, and each was 'boss of something'. He never asked for volunteers. A man would be chosen for a particular job and then left to use his own judgement in carrying it out. When orders came from Watkins they were usually disguised by 'would you mind . . .?'. He would demonstrate his fitness for the role of leader by learning faster than the others and by his unmatched appetite for work. Watkins once said that he had never felt tired.

The expedition sailed from St Katherine's Dock, London, on 6 July 1930. The *Quest*, chartered with captain and crew from a Norwegian seal-hunting company, had taken part in the search for General Nobile, and was Sir Ernest Shackleton's last ship – in fact he died on board, in the cabin now occupied by Gino Watkins and August Courtauld. At Gravesend a farewell lunch was held aboard the yacht of their principal sponsor, Major Stephen Courtauld, during which his pet lemur bit the expedition's wireless operator – 'a deep bite in the wrist which bled all over the upper deck and made an awful mess on the beautiful new planking'. The first casualty stitched and bandaged, the *Quest* proceeded into open waters under a flag showing a polar bear with wings.

Most of the men were in their bunks when the *Quest* entered the pack ice that drifts south along the coast of Greenland. They heard the ship's engine repeatedly stop and restart, punctuated by alarming bumps. Above decks, the captain – in a bowler hat he always wore in times of danger – was shouting instructions from the crow's-nest. He was threading his way through to the tiny Danish settlement of Angmagssalik.

Around them the brilliant blue water was 'covered with lumps of dazzling white ice of all shapes and sizes'. As they neared the shore, a small flotilla of Eskimo kayaks paddled frantically to greet them.

Base camp was established in a fjord thirty miles from Angmagssalik. The site Watkins chose offered reasonable shelter, good conditions for radio, clear water for the Gypsy Moths, and access, via a glacier, to the ice cap. For two weeks the men worked long shifts ferrying supplies and equipment to the shore, including the heavy timber needed to build the hut Watkins had designed. Martin Lindsay, of the Royal Scots Fusiliers, found the work 'exceedingly unpleasant', having 'seldom previously carried anything heavier than a message'. Later he was grateful for the level of physical fitness he quickly achieved.

As soon as the base hut was built and the Gypsy Moths assembled and tested, Watkins sent a surveying party northwards along the coast and a sledging party on to the inland ice. The meteorological station was to be set up immediately. Of the men chosen for the task only one, J. M. Scott, had driven a dog sled before. The others were obliged to learn by trial and error: dogs pulled in different directions, then became entangled in their traces; hands were bitten, sledges overturned, men accidentally whipped themselves in the face – but all were competent dog-handlers before they returned. By the end of the expedition, the most confident of them wondered why Robert Peary had considered it an arcane skill best left to the Eskimos.

Every sledging party destined for the ice cap during the course of the expedition had first to contend with a long slope at the foot of the glacier. A sheet of ice as smooth as glass, pitched at a demoralising gradient, it became known as Buggery Bank. Eventually a block and tackle were used to haul heavy sledges to the top; the challenge of scaling it on foot was likened by Lindsay to a game of snakes and ladders. He watched a man ahead of him slip: 'Suddenly he started to come down – head first; sliding on his stomach he tore past me, with a look of pained surprise on his face.'

The party establishing the ice-cap station took six days to travel fifteen miles from the base. As the area of ridges, pools and crevasses receded, and the slope became a plateau, so travelling became easier and their sledging speeds increased. 'The dark tops of the coastal mountains gradually disappeared below an encircling horizon of snow,' wrote Spencer Chapman. From then on, 'No rock or patch of earth nor any living thing broke the monotony.' The next 112 miles – to the position chosen for station – were made in only ten days. They were by now more than 8000 feet above sea level, at what seemed to be the maximum elevation of the ice cap.

The 'station' was a dome-shaped tent, ten feet in diameter, suspended from a curved bamboo frame over which a second tent was hung. The air-space between the two skins provided insulation. A ventilation tube emerged from the apex of the roof, giving the station, Chapman noticed, the appearance of an outsized umbrella. Like an igloo, the tent was entered through a tunnel built below floor level, preventing the escape of warm air. An array of meteorological instruments was erected outside, including maximum and minimum thermometers, a cup anemometer to measure wind-speed and a comb nephescope to determine the rate at which clouds passed. Martin Lindsay and Quintin Riley were the first to man the station.

After the intense activity of the previous few weeks, they welcomed the calm routine of meteorological work. 'This funny little dwelling,' wrote Lindsay, 'was a very happy home for us, and Riley and I look back on the days we spent there as being amongst the most enjoyable of the whole expedition.' There was time for chess, and for watching the sun set beautifully on the blank horizon. 'The stillness is unbroken save for the flapping of the flag as the wind comes and goes, and sometimes the sighing of the snow as it speeds along the ground.' The northern lights reminded Lieutenant Lindsay of 'a muster of dim lances, close serried, standing erect in the sky'.

They had forgotten to pack an alarm clock. It had been planned to take readings from the instruments at three-hourly intervals through day and night, but the unpopular night shifts were now abandoned. A Union Jack was flown, and two adjoining snowhouses built (with an ease that surprised them) according to the directions in *The Friendly Arctic*. Books of less practical relevance kept 'mental stagnation' at bay: when the small collection of Victorian novels ran out, the men on the ice cap could read Socrates' *Discourses* and Fowler's *English Usage*. If prolonged isolation led to a craving for facts and statistics from the civilised world, there was a copy of *Whitaker's Almanack*.

Stephenson's surveying party returned from its northward journey in mid-September, having mapped as far north as Kangerdlugsuak Fjord. They had used a combination of the *Quest*, open boats and one of the

Gypsy Moths. Favourable ice conditions had enabled the *Quest* to penetrate Kangerdlugsuak; it had never previously been navigated. The aeroplane took off from an area of clear water, and from it Watkins saw a range of mountains, sixty miles to the north, 'whose very existence had never been suspected'. They were of 'Himalayan grandeur', estimated at between 15,000 and 17,000 feet (this was later revised to 12,000). The Danish administrators of Greenland later named them the Watkins Mountains.

Up on the ice cap, temperatures were falling rapidly. Lindsay's diary recorded the September nights as 'chilly', 'cold', then 'damnably cold'. By the time they were relieved and replaced on 2 October they had recorded a low of -35 °C and were wondering if their thermometers might not go low enough to measure winter temperatures. Sledging conditions were deteriorating. Autumn winds drove a mist of loose snow across the ice, making it difficult to follow the trail of flag-poles between the station and the base. Returning from the ice cap, Lindsay and Riley's party spent three days waiting for blizzards to abate. Their discomfort was increased when Lindsay – 'not having a mechanical mind' – decided to use the paraffin tin as a chopping board for the frozen dog pemmican. His other tool was an axe. 'The experiment was an entire success as far as the dog pemmican was concerned, but unfortunately the tin split too and most of our precious paraffin supply ran away into the snow.' The remaining nights were spent in unheated tents.

Back at Base Fjord, Lindsay and Riley were introduced to the expedition's latest recruits. Three Eskimo girls had been taken on to work at the hut, as servants and seamstresses. They slept – or were supposed to sleep – in the loft, and earned two cigarettes a day. Arpika was 'the oldest and most sensible of the girls' and Gertrude 'the prettiest, who expected to be made a fuss of and at first only worked when she felt like it'. Tina 'was once seen blowing her nose on somebody's sleeping bag . . . and had a habit of spitting on the dirty plates and then rubbing them with her fingers, so she was usually known to us as the "little slut".' Before long, however, they had been taught the correct way to serve at table: 'they brought the dishes round to the left side as if they had been doing it all their lives.'

After the exciting discoveries of the coastal journey and the successful establishment of the ice-cap station, the mood in the base hut was buoyant. It was enlivened by the presence of the girls, who pampered the young men and were fond of the gramophone. When the girls played their favourite record once too often it was thrown out of the window, but they retrieved the pieces and sewed them together with sealskin.

Eventually there was some antagonism in the base over Arpika, Gertrude and Tina, between the men who liked to sleep with them (including Chapman and Watkins) and those who did not (including Lindsay and Courtauld). Courtauld in particular did not like being climbed over during the night by a girl making her way to Watkins' bunk.

Watkins wished he had designed a larger hut. However, if these resentments became open disputes they were not recorded, and a spirit of good humour seems to have prevailed. Lindsay attributed the 'lack of trouble' to the adaptability of youth and to the similarity of their backgrounds:

> We had all much the same way of thinking. Ten of us were
> Cambridge men and three out of the remaining four were service
> officers. We had no member of the so-called 'working classes',
> and no 'hard case'.

Before returning to Norway, the *Quest* made a return trip to Iceland to collect ski undercarriage for the Gypsy Moths, which De Havilland had mistakenly omitted from the aeroplane crates. It was an unexpected opportunity for each of the men to add their needs to the shopping list. Courtauld had a craving for suet, and radioed home a request for some to be sent to Reykjavik – but the package he received from his mother contained a suit.

On 26 October Chapman and Courtauld set off from the base hut for the ice cap, in a large sledging party. It was time to relieve the men at the ice station and to bring enough supplies to last the next occupants until the end of March. Further relief journeys would not be possible in the winter months. There was a possibility that the Gypsy Moths, once fitted with skis, would be able to fly over the ice cap and land at the station if conditions proved favourable, but this could not be relied upon. Heavy radio equipment was packed on the sledges with the intention of setting it up at the station – Watkins hoped to maintain contact with the men during what might be a long period of isolation. This alone weighed 600 pounds. The total load on the sledges worked out at more than 100 pounds per dog.

Six days were spent hauling the sledges up Buggery Bank. Soon after reaching the top they were pinned down by a ferocious blizzard, and by 5 November they had travelled just ten miles in eleven days. The next day Chapman wrote in his diary:

Gale continued with increasing violence all night and day. Our tents simply can't last much longer. The dogs have all bitten free and are huddled against the tent for protection . . . it is impossible to breathe with this wind . . . in the evening the gale became ghastly and we put our clothes on inside our bags in readiness. We could not hear each other speak and hoarfrost poured over us like snow. The wind must be well over 100 m.p.h. It must have felt rather like this being under shellfire during the war. If the tent goes we are corpses.

On 10 November, having travelled fifteen miles in fifteen days, they met Watkins and Scott returning from a 100-mile southward journey. It was an extraordinary coincidence in poor visibility. Watkins doubted that they would reach the station with enough supplies intact for two men to remain there. 'Do the best you can,' he told Chapman. 'You may have to abandon the station. But at all costs you must get the two men out.' Chapman was left to make up his own mind. He decided to dump the radio equipment and send half of the party back; he would press on with Courtauld and Wager.

When the wind subsided they found the surface of the ice cap had been 'lashed . . . into a maze of frozen ripples and waves'. Marble-hard, the ridges frequently overturned or damaged the sledges. At night, it would take all three men to unroll Chapman's frozen sleeping bag. Each was suffering from frostbite:

The ends of our fingers are all hard and insensitive. The toes . . . are very painful now and keep me awake. The nails have dropped off and the big toes are raw and stick to my socks.

The dogs amazed Chapman: though weakened by the dreadful conditions, and miserable at night, they continued to pull all day. When their commands were ignored, the men were obliged to be brutal: 'One behaves like an animal and hits them anywhere with any weapon. However they seem quite impervious to punishment either from us or from each other.' On 21 November Chapman killed the weakest of them with the blunt side of his axe. Two days later a bitch in Courtauld's team produced a puppy:

> *Dreng (the father) licked the snow off it. We relentlessly fed it to another team, and the same had to be done with three other puppies which appeared in turn each time we stopped. Yet the bitch pulled well between each. Poor brute, but what else could we do?*

It was not until 3 December, after thirty-eight days of sledging, that Chapman, Courtauld and Wager arrived at the ice-cap station. The temperature was -41°C. They shouted 'Evening Standard! Evening Standard!' at the entrance to the tunnel, and the two very relieved occupants emerged. Chapman's party was three weeks late.

During a few days of recuperation for the sledging party, the five men discussed what should be done with the station. There were insufficient rations for two men to remain there until spring. Nobody wanted to abandon the station, as this would mean the failure of one of the main programmes of the expedition, and yet the alternative, to leave a man there alone, when relief might not come until March or April, seemed unsafe and unfair – except to August Courtauld, who had already made up his mind that he rather liked the idea. The men who had been there since 2 October tried to talk him out of it. They told him about the strange effects of their isolation: one had been suddenly terrified by the loud flapping of the Union Jack, and bolted for the tent. The other had run away from a weather instrument having mistaken it for a mysterious human intruder. The phlegmatic Courtauld was unimpressed: 'As I had frostbite in my toes, I had no wish to make the journey back.' He wrote a letter for Watkins explaining that he stayed behind on his own responsibility. After an improvised Christmas dinner, they left Courtauld to his solitary winter vigil on 6 December.

At the base hut Scott celebrated Christmas Day by running naked in the snow. On New Year's Eve they were remembered by BBC radio: 'We have a message for the British Arctic Air Route Expedition, in Greenland's icy mountains, who listen to our news every day. Good luck to them!' However, the flying schedule planned for the winter had to be cancelled after a series of accidents. On 4 January a gale overturned and severely damaged one of the aircraft; the tail plain was eventually reconstructed using driftwood and the fabric of a shirt. The other Gypsy Moth flew over the ice cap on 20 February, but it proved impossible to find the station from the air amongst the ridges and shadows created by the winter winds; the next day this aircraft too was out of action after hitting an ice-ridge on landing. The demonstration flight to Winnipeg was now cancelled. The ferocity of gales on the coast surprised them. One of the anemometers measured 129 m.p.h. before it was blown away.

During the short winter days the men learned to hunt. *The Friendly Arctic* contained practical advice on the stalking of seals. Watkins tried two methods of getting within rifle-range. One was to dress in black, lie on the ice, mimic the seals' habit of raising the head to scan the horizon, and creep slowly towards them. The other, which he found to be more comfortable, was to advance behind a white cloth screen that disguised him as a piece of ice. Only a small number were shot; most of the seals eaten at the base hut that winter were bought from the Eskimos, who hunted from kayaks. Watkins decided that when the summer came his men would learn to use the sealskin canoes.

With the failure to reach Courtauld by air, the relief of the station by a sledging party – at the first sign of reasonable weather – became the expedition's priority. On 9 March, after two abortive attempts, Scott, Riley and Lindsay set out from the base hut.

Two weeks later Watkins flew once more over the ice cap but saw no sign of the station, nor of Scott's party. Late at night on 17 April Scott returned with bad news. He did not have Courtauld with him. He had reached the vicinity of the station but had found no trace of it. Without a wireless time-signal set, Scott had been unable to determine his longitude, and therefore their precise position, but latitude observations and dead reckoning had told them they were within a few miles, and should have been able to see it. For three weeks they had remained in the area, searching on every day the weather allowed. Eventually Scott had decided to return, in order to save the dogs for a second attempt.

Stephenson checked through their navigational data and confirmed that they had passed within one mile of the station's position. Only two explanations were possible: either Scott's party had somehow failed to see it, or it could not be seen because it had been completely – and permanently – buried under the drifting snow. Scott might have walked over Courtauld's tomb without knowing.

Watkins showed no emotion. 'He did not seem either pleased or angry, excited or disappointed by what I told him,' wrote Scott; 'merely interested.' According to Lindsay, Watkins took no part in the discussions 'on the possibilities or probabilities of some disaster having occurred at the ice-cap station . . . he was convinced that Courtauld was all right, and nothing could shake his faith.'

If Courtauld were alive, he would soon be at the limit of his rations. On 21 April, in the first clear weather since Scott's return, Watkins set off for the ice cap with Chapman and Rymill. Before he left, Watkins had sent a message to the expedition committee in London, explaining to them that Scott's party had been unable to locate the station in conditions of poor visibility, and that he, personally, was leaving at once with five weeks of sledging rations. The message concluded: 'There is always the possibility that Courtauld is not alive, or unwell, in which case station is probably completely covered.' Amongst his sledging equipment Watkins had packed a prayer book.

Inevitably the message caused great alarm in Courtauld's family and horrified his fiancée, Mollie Montgomery. She had agreed to marry him shortly before the expedition left London. His father was on board the *Queen Mary*, in mid-Atlantic, when he heard the news; he instructed that no expense should be spared if there was anything that could be done to help. The committee decided to charter an aeroplane. The Swedish pilot Captain Ahrenberg knew there was no prospect of seeing the station from the air, but his large Junkers monoplane was capable of remaining airborne far longer than the expedition's Gypsy Moths. This would give him a better chance of spotting a sledging party on the ice; extra rations could then be dropped, and the time spent searching for Courtauld extended. Watkins knew nothing of this when he left for the ice cap, and nothing of the sensational stories that began to appear in the British press.

'ARCTIC AIR QUEST FOR AN EXPLORER – MILLIONAIRE'S SON ALONE ON ICE' was the headline of the *Daily Express*. According to the paper, 'the search now being made in the Arctic . . . is dramatic in its intensity'. The *Daily Herald* imagined 'the eyes of a starving man, marooned alone in his tiny snow-hut on the lofty ice cap of Greenland . . . gladdened by the sight of an aeroplane swooping from the east'.

Misunderstanding – or distorting – the purpose of Ahrenberg's mission, the *Evening Standard* announced that Watkins' relief party was also missing. It was 'a further disastrous development'. The same paper invented a desperate wireless message transmitted by Courtauld: '*Absolutely without food*'. There was, of course, no radio equipment at the ice-cap station. In a French newspaper, Augustine Courtauld was assumed to be a woman.

In London the expedition committee published its views in *The Times*, which had bought exclusive rights to the explorers' reports from Greenland. It expected Watkins' relief party to locate the station. There was 'no cause for alarm'. The committee had 'seen in certain newspapers reports about the expedition which are inaccurate and in some cases without foundation and which are likely to cause unnecessary anxiety'. At the base hut the wireless operator received a message from a mysterious Professor Johannesson, announcing that he was on his way, with a seaplane, aboard the Icelandic patrol vessel *Odinn*. He had a bizarre question for the wireless operator: 'What is Courtauld looking for?' Johannesson claimed to be acting on the authority of the committee secretary, but suspicions were aroused when it was learned from Angmagssalik that there was a reporter aboard the *Odinn*. The base contacted London at once: 'Who is Professor Johannesson and who told him to come?' The committee replied that it had never heard of him.

Sledging conditions were good for Watkins' journey. On 5 May, in bright, clear weather, observations for latitude and longitude placed the men a mile north-west of the station; these calculations were considered to be accurate within a few hundred yards. Advancing with dogs on leads, in the hope that they might detect the scent of the station, they suddenly saw a black speck in front of them. It proved to be the remains of the Union Jack. They had found the ice-cap station. Chapman was elated.

> But as we got near we began to have certain misgivings. The whole place had a most extraordinary air of desolation . . . only the tops of the various survey instruments and the handle of a spade projected through the vast snowdrift, which submerged the whole tent with its snow houses and surrounding wall. Was it possible that a man could be alive there?

A few inches of the ventilator pipe protruded from the surface. Watkins shouted down the pipe. 'Imagine our joy and relief when an answering shout came faintly from the depths of the snow. The voice was tremulous, but it was the voice of a normal man.' Within a few moments Watkins had dug down to the roof of the tent and cut through the fabric, and Courtauld, bearded like 'a prophet', his hollow face black with soot, climbed out into the glaring sunshine.

Laconic and self-contained, August Courtauld never had a great deal to say about his five months of solitude. In December it had appealed to him as an experiment. Privately, he was tired of the close-quarters of the base hut and of the relentless physical work of sledging. He described himself as lazy and irritable, but he was also immensely strong-minded and resourceful. Of all the men in the party, Stephenson believed that only Courtauld 'could have done what he did and come out absolutely mentally alert and physically well'.

Alone, what struck him first was the absolute silence of the ice cap. When the wind died, 'the only thing you could hear was the blood pounding in your ears'. At first he found his clothes were infested with lice, having lent his sleeping bag to one of the girls at the base. He left his clothes on the ice for a fortnight: 'This seemed to do them in.' They were the last living creatures he saw before Watkins and Chapman arrived five months later. 'I never saw a bird, or even a fly.'

> One day in February a queer thing happened. I was lying in my sleeping bag when suddenly I heard a noise like an underground train coming. The noise ended in a mighty crash. I thought that the whole station might have dropped into a crevasse; however, everything seemed to be all right. When I had got over it sufficiently, I ventured out to see what had happened. To my amazement, everything looked exactly as before.

Courtauld had to clear the tunnel of snow each time he ventured out to read the instruments. It was becoming more difficult each day as the drifts around the tent grew deeper. One evening he made the elementary mistake of leaving his spade outside, and awoke to find the tunnel blocked. Another exit was made through the roof of the adjoining snow-house, but this too drifted over: 'I was then imprisoned.' For the last five weeks he remained so, the tent shrinking under the weight of snow, icicles gradually extending towards his face. He could no longer spare fuel for the reading lamp, and lay in the dark. At first Courtauld feared he would never be rescued, but rather than giving way to panic, a strange feeling of security came over him:

> as time went on, I began to feel complete confidence. I knew
> that, even if Gino was having to wait for better weather, he
> wouldn't let me down. I began to realise that I would not be left
> to die. I came to know that I was held by the Everlasting Arms.

On the day that Watkins arrived, Courtauld used his last drop of paraffin.

As Watkins, Chapman, Rymill and Courtauld made their way back towards the base, a large Junkers monoplane swooped over them and dropped parcels of food – which they did not need. They had no idea where it came from. Captain Ahrenberg, having seen four men on the ice, knew that Courtauld had been found. The information was soon relayed to London and to the newspapers. Mollie Montgomery would not believe the good news until she read it in *The Times*. When the rescue of Courtauld became a newsreel feature, she went from cinema to cinema to watch over and again the pictures of her fiancée emerging safe and well from his hole in the ice.

It was not until Watkins and Courtauld reached the base hut that they became aware of the publicity surrounding the expedition. They were furious. In Watkins' view, outside assistance was never needed. He felt the drama played out in the newspapers, with its implication that the expedition had got itself into serious difficulties, reflected badly on his leadership. Courtauld was embarrassed to discover he had been cast as the hero.

Before the men returned to England, several great journeys were made in order to complete the work of the expedition. The ice cap was traversed along two routes to the western and southern coasts of Greenland. Wager and Stephenson climbed Mount Ferol to a height of over 11,000 feet; nobody had climbed higher in the Arctic, and though Wager was an experienced mountaineer, Stephenson had never climbed before.

The men learned to handle kayaks, to roll upright when they

capsized, and to shoot seals from them. The most remarkable and most perilous journey of all was a 700-mile voyage in open whaleboats around the southern tip of Greenland by Watkins, Chapman and a somewhat reluctant Courtauld. He was tired of the perpetual discomfort of his year in Greenland, and eager to return to his fiancée. Watkins took his kayak on the whaleboat, and the men depended for their food on his newly acquired skills as a hunter.

It was widely recognised as the most fruitful British Arctic expedition for fifty years. Many miles of coastline and a new range of mountains were added to the map of Greenland, and much of the mystery removed from the ice cap. For the first time, a British expedition had successfully adapted to Eskimo methods of travel and hunting. Another twenty years would pass before Scandinavian Airline Systems inaugurated a trans-polar route for commercial flights to the western coast of the USA, but Watkins' prediction that it would eventually become commonplace has been proved right.

He was awarded the Gold Medals of the Geographical Societies of Britain, Norway and Denmark. It seemed that the young explorer had the world – albeit a rapidly shrinking world – at his feet. But he was unable to find adequate financial backing for his next proposal, a cross-ing of Antarctica, and in 1932 returned once more to east Greenland with Chapman, Riley and Rymill. On 20 August Gino Watkins went out in his kayak to hunt seals, and never returned. The canoe was found, waterlogged and drifting, and on a nearby ice-floe, his trousers and spray-skirt. It was impossible to judge how the accident had happened: he may have capsized while shooting, or been attacked by a bladder-nosed seal he had wounded. He may have been on the ice-floe, looking for seals, when a glacier 'calved' a berg, sending a wave across the fjord that tipped his kayak into the water. However he came to be separated from his kayak, Watkins seems to have chosen to remove his trousers and swim after it, rather than wait to be rescued. Chapman knew Watkins would have thought it 'ignominious to be found stranded on a lump of ice'. The water was a few degrees below freezing, and Watkins was prone to cramp. 'There are many sharks about,' wrote Chapman, 'and we knew we would have little hope of finding the body.'

Had Watkins survived Greenland, his friend Scott believed he would have died as a fighter pilot in the war – his love of flying and his lack of fear would eventually have been his undoing. Chapman famously survived his war, writing *The Jungle is Neutral* about his experiences in Malaysia. August Courtauld married Mollie Montgomery, and died of multiple sclerosis in 1959; his widow later married the Conservative minister Rab Butler. Lady Butler of Saffron Walden still lives in the beautiful house she originally shared with Courtauld. She says the weeks of waiting for news of his fate, as he lay entombed in the Greenland ice, scarred her for life: 'For ever afterwards I used to expect awful things to happen.' Alfred Stephenson, the youngest member of the expedition, is its only survivor. 'I've always kept a spade inside the door,' he says, 'even in Wiltshire.'

Chapter Eight

THE WAR FOR THE WEATHER

There were no major battles, no epic encounters of planes or tanks, no headlines in the home-town newspapers. Loneliness doesn't rate a citation; they don't give medals for waiting. The casualties were not very glamorous: frozen lungs, a couple of missing fingers or toes, an amputated leg. We were not fighting to defeat a division or capture a ridge. It was not a war for territory. It was a war for the weather.

Bernt Balchen, *War Below Zero*

High up in the mountains above Singnehamna and buried under rocks on Nordauestlandet far above the Arctic Circle, you can still find the remains of a top secret German operation from the Second World War. Though many of the participants are now dead and the details of the story are slowly fading away in military archives, the rusting barrels, broken sledges and smashed radio valves still exist to tell the tale. Between 1940 and 1945 twelve elite expeditions were dispatched to the Arctic under orders to set up weather stations for the Luftwaffe and the German Navy. They faced an equally determined group of former miners, scientists and explorers who were sent north by the Allies to frustrate the German plans and bring back their own weather information. For the first time in its history, the Arctic was dragged into a modern war.

The weather has played a crucial role in individual battles, but it wasn't until this century that advance weather information became a critical factor in military planning. In February 1942 the German ships *Gneisenau*, *Prinz Eugene* and *Scharnhorst* took advantage of a severe fog to make a daring daylight escape from Brest in France up to the North Sea, under the noses of the British guns at Dover. In December

1944 German commanders planned the Ardennes offensive around the information given to them by their meteorological staff. They waited until they were forecast three days of terrible weather before they began the operation. Allied planes were virtually grounded and the Germans made huge advances. However, on the fourth the weather changed and the German advance was halted. In both of these examples, weather information from the Arctic played a decisive role in the final timing of the operations. The Arctic is Europe's 'weather kitchen' and both the Allies and the Axis powers were willing to put tremendous efforts into gathering their own information and denying their opponents.

The opening shots in the Arctic campaign were fired on 9 April 1940 when a fleet of German ships steamed into Oslofjord in Norway. The battle was brief but bloody, and by the next day Oslo had fallen. Two days later Germany invaded Denmark, and by June both countries were in German hands. Each had extensive territories in the Arctic: Norway had been awarded the islands of the Svalbard archipelago in 1920 by an international treaty and Greenland had been recognised as a Danish colony since 1933. Now with the mainland conquered, the people in the Arctic wondered what would happen next. In Greenland's case, the Danish governor decided that he would not co-operate with the Germans; one of his first acts was to cease transmitting weather reports back to Germany. Within four months the Germans sent an undercover team to east Greenland to set up a secret weather station. In response, the Danes created their famous 'sledge-patrols', made up of former trappers and hunters, whose job was to defend several hundred miles of the eastern coastline. The Danish governor turned to the USA for help, and long before they formally declared war on Germany American ice-breakers were patrolling Greenland's Arctic waters.

The most intense activity of the war took place on Spitsbergen, the largest island in the Svalbard archipelago. It had been discovered in the late sixteenth century by the Dutch explorer William Barents. For years Svalbard remained an entrepreneurial no man's land with various French and British whaling fleets battling for fishing rights. When the fish stocks had been depleted, the money men turned their eyes to the island's mineral potential and in the early part of this century there was a veritable coal rush, with various British and American prospectors descending on Spitsbergen to set up mining operations. When Svalbard was awarded to Norway, they had to agree that it would remain a demilitarised zone. Bolshevik Russia had not been invited to sign the treaty and indeed the Soviet government questioned Norwegian sovereignty and maintained a strong presence on Spitsbergen. At the outbreak of war, there were about 2500 Norwegians and Russians on the island, most of them miners. When Norway fell, coal production continued, but in June 1941, after the invasion of Russia, the Allies considered occupying the island and diverting production to Britain and Russia. Instead they decided to evacuate Spitsbergen and disable the mines.

A large passenger liner, the *Empress of Canada*, was sent up to Barentsburg, the main Russian settlement, with a detachment of Canadian troops and an official from the Soviet embassy in London. It was supposed to be a top secret operation, but when they arrived in Barentsburg they found out that *Operation Gauntlet* had been known about for several days. No one was too keen to leave, but grudgingly queues began forming at the quayside and the ship soon filled up with miners and their families. Then, for some inexplicable reason, the Russian consul decided that he didn't want to leave without an official order from Moscow and began broadcasting his objections on the town's loudspeaker system. The British officer in charge of the evacuation tried to be in turn sympathetic, diplomatic and forceful, but all to no avail. Finally noticing that the consul was very proud of his wine cellar and his supplies of Russian brandy, the officer lured him into a drinking match until he was carried on board on a stretcher, blind drunk. To avoid any possible recriminations, several photographs were taken of the consul in his inebriated state; whether any similar photographs were taken of the British officer was not mentioned in dispatches.

Canadian sappers quickly set to work destroying most of the mining infrastructure though the mine-shafts themselves were left intact. Meanwhile the remainder of the task force moved up to Longyearbyen, the main Norwegian settlement. Initially there was some resistance to the evacuation plan: some people felt that if they stopped sending coal back to Norway, it would only make matters worse on the mainland. Others just didn't like the idea of leaving. There was a strong community feeling on Spitsbergen coupled with a fierce individualism in many of the people who had settled there. Eventually, after several town meetings, the evacuation went ahead on 2 September.

During the operation, the Allies had broadcast fake weather reports to the Norwegian mainland, claiming that the area was covered by low cloud in order to deter any German visitors. When transmissions abruptly stopped, the Luftwaffe sent a plane to investigate. They saw the smoke from burning coal stocks at Barentsburg many miles away. When the plane flew over Longyearbyen it was clearly deserted save for one solitary figure: a die-hard Norwegian trapper who had refused to be evacuated and had hidden under a pier. The Germans had no choice now but to set up their own weather station; the Allies had already occupied Iceland and Jan Mayen Land, two islands further south, and with Spitsbergen evacuated they had no other source of weather data. By the beginning of October weather station *Banso* was operating from a small hut close to the German landing strip. Three weeks later, British mine-sweepers returned to Spitsbergen and attacked the German position. The meteorologists fled, but returned a month later and remained there throughout the winter.

As the war intensified, the strategic importance of Spitsbergen grew. In the late summer of 1941 the Allies sent the first of a series of vital convoys to Russia. Before long, there were two convoys a month braving the North Sea en route to the Soviet ports on the Kola Peninsula. The sea between the top of Norway and the bottom of Spitsbergen was a crucial choke point on this journey where Allied convoys were particularly vulnerable to attacks by U-boats and planes. There were several German air-bases on the Norwegian mainland and the Allies feared that their next step would be to set up airfields on Spitsbergen and attack the convoys from two sides. When British agents in Sweden seized confidential documents which implied that the Germans were just about to step up their activities on Spitsbergen, the Allies decided to act. A plan was hatched to re-occupy the island, though no one was quite sure at this stage how many Germans were stationed there.

In April 1942 the Allies began aerial reconnaissance to ascertain the full extent of the German presence on the island. Flying from bases on Shetland, British Catalina seaplanes made the perilous 2700-mile return flight. At first they saw no sign of any human presence at all, but on 13 May a Heinkel aeroplane was spotted on the ground and machine-gunned. Even as they turned back to warn Allied Command that the Germans were on the island, two Norwegian ships were braving their way through minefields north of Iceland, heading for Spitsbergen. The eighty Norwegians and three British liaison officers on board the ship never got the message. Most of the Norwegians were former miners who were chosen for *Operation Fritham* because of their first-hand knowledge of Spitsbergen. It was a top secret operation: they had travelled through Britain dressed as sailors and had not been told where they were going, but when they arrived on the quayside at Greenock in Scotland and saw the piles of skis and sheepskin sleeping bags they guessed what was afoot.

On 13 May they arrived aboard two ships, the *Isbjorn* and the *Selis*, at Isfjorden, the large fjord outside Barentsburg. For most of their journey conditions had been good, but now they were faced with solid ice blocking their way into the harbour. Patrols were sent across the ice to Cape Linne and Barentsburg while the ships slowly attempted to break their way through the pack. Early in the day, two unknown planes were seen far away on the horizon but the Norwegian commander refused to evacuate the ships. They had been spotted and that evening four Focke-Wulf Kondors paid them a visit which they never forgot. Atle Gresli was on board the *Selis*:

> About half an hour elapsed before we heard the first engine sounds. The noise got louder and louder but we couldn't see anything because they were flying in front of the sun, then we saw two planes coming in very low, less than a hundred metres above the ice. I saw a bomb drop from the plane, it landed right in front of the bow of the Isbjorn and a second later it looked as if the ship had been lifted into the air. Its two huge, thick steel masts snapped like matchsticks.

The *Isbjorn* sank within minutes, and soon the *Selis* was burning out of control. Then the Germans came back for more. For almost an hour they strafed and bombed the men who had somehow managed to get off the ships. Hans Iversen remembers how they lay there 'like seals'; Atle Gresli saw his comrades killed and this quiet man learned how to hate:

> As we lay there on the ice, I was terrified, I was almost hysterical with fear. But after the planes had flown over a couple of times, I suddenly became furious. I lay there swearing and cursing and had I got hold of a German at that point I'd have killed him with my bare hands, that's for sure. I think that

was what saved me, I didn't go into shock or anything like that
afterwards. I became so angry, I'd never been that angry before,
I felt so helpless.

Paradoxically, the ice also provided some protection for the re-occupation force. Sir Alexander Glen, a former explorer, was one of the three British liaison officers attached to the expedition:

We were damn lucky to be hit on the ice – had the attack been
in open sea no one would have survived. They made a mistake
in dropping their bombs too low, probably 700 feet, and the
bombs in fact bounced on the ice, usually two or three times,
and the bounce was long enough to give you that opportunity
of just moving a bit to the left or the right to avoid them.

After forty-five minutes the German planes left. Fourteen men were dead, including the commander of the expedition, Einar Sverdrup. The Norwegians regrouped in Barentsburg and attended to their wounded as best they could. Most of their supplies had gone down with the two ships, they had few guns and little food. Unfortunately, when Barentsburg had been evacuated no medicines were left in the hospital, but a number of doctors' coats were now liberated to be used for camouflage. Stranger still were the discoveries made by other search parties. Sir Alexander Glen had been part of the evacuation force in 1941 and luckily he had a good memory:

Food which one might guess was the first concern was in fact
the last, because when we evacuated we'd killed thirty or forty
pigs at a farm and they were all still in a snowdrift, perfectly
preserved à la Tesco or Safeways, so we had endless supplies of
pork. The real lucky dip were boxes of Russian dried
mushrooms from the Steppes – they were a joy – and we had a
rather good supply of sticky Russian sweets.

The Norwegians had lost all their wireless equipment but they were confident that eventually planes would be sent out from Britain to investigate. Two men were sent to Cape Heer at the tip of Isfjorden to wait for their arrival. They improvised an Aldis lamp and finally, thirteen days after the attack, a Catalina arrived. 'Sure enough the sortie was flown, over came the Catalina and spotted us and we exchanged signals. The surprise was from their side, us not saying "Evacuation please, crisis", but "We want arms, we want to be re-equipped, we're sticking here".'

In the following two weeks there were several further flights, evacuating the wounded and bringing in vital supplies and weapons. In July two British naval ships arrived with reinforcements and a new Norwegian commander, Ernst Ullring. He had already distinguished himself in Greenland and was determined to take the fight to the enemy. Alexander Glen will never forget him:

> I don't think defence ever came into his thoughts, he lived for attack, he had the Nelson touch – by God, he had. He did have some regrettable habits – the Germans dropped a lot of anti-personnel bombs, and he used to tuck unexploded ones under his left arm; he always smoked a pipe and he would be chatting with you, he'd be knocking out his pipe on the fuse of the shell.

The Norwegians prepared themselves to mount an attack on Longyearbyen, which they thought contained the main German garrison, but by the time they arrived it had been evacuated. They did manage to shoot down a Ju-88 whose crew included Eric Etienne, the leader of *Operation Banso*, who ironically had been a member of two Oxford University expeditions to Greenland in the late thirties. The Norwegians set up their own weather station and were transmitting reports to Britain by the end of November.

They were now largely in control of the island, but they still had to put up with German bombers, which came up to six times a day. Toralf Lund was a member of one of the Norwegian sledge patrols:

> When we were out patrolling we left a lot of ski traces in all different directions in the snow, so that Germans flying over wouldn't know where we were going. We sometimes had to sleep outside in tents. One night the lieutenant's beard froze on to his sleeping bag so we had to cut him free with a bayonet – we had no scissors. He screamed like a baby.

November saw one of the cruellest episodes in the whole campaign when a British merchant ship, the *Chulmleigh*, ran aground on the south coast of Spitsbergen. The crew of fifty-eight men abandoned ship and clambered into two lifeboats. They had few provisions and were desperately short of water; no one had any real hope that they would survive. John Swainston was one of the sailors who was aboard the second lifeboat:

> *We discovered that two of the seamen we had believed were dozing at the bottom of the boat were dead and it took all our strength to lift the corpses and throw them overboard. Next day the steward tore off all his clothes, staring at us unseeingly and shouting. He had gone mad with thirst. We tried to quieten him but his crazy strength was too much for us. He fought his way towards the side of the boat and fell into the sea. Within seconds he was out of sight.*

On the fourth day they were amazed to sight land and managed somehow to get ashore. They found a lonely hut in which the Norwegians had cached some emergency supplies. Twenty-six men landed, but within four days thirteen men had died of frostbite and exposure. They remained there for almost two months, not realising that the Norwegians were only a few miles away. In another hut they found a sack of flour which was their only source of food for several weeks until it too ran out. 'In a tin about the size of a biscuit box, we found a hunk of putrid meat. I think it was seal, it stank. We cut it up into slices and hung it up outside to freeze. We rationed ourselves to one cube a day of this flesh. It tasted foul but we were keeping death at bay.'

Then suddenly, on 2 January, two members of a Norwegian patrol from Barentsburg came upon the hut. They had no idea what was going on, so whilst one of them lay on the snow covering his comrade, the other gingerly approached the doorway. Inside he found an extraordinary scene: 'He thought they were negroes. They had found some oil and they put a bit of cloth in it and used that as a fryer, but there was so much smoke that they ended up black.'

Two of the sailors were taken back to Barentsburg, but the full horror of the scene only became clear when Leif Andreasson returned with two other Norwegians to rescue the remaining men.

I remember we had to go into that hut and carry all the people

*out, a lot of them were frozen to death. It is difficult to say how
many there were, you could see that foxes had been eating
some of the bodies. It was dark – you didn't see too much, you
didn't feel too much, you had a job to do.*

Nine men were taken back to town but many of them were suffering
from severe frostbite. Toralf Lund was assigned to assist the doctor: 'We
had to amputate fingers and toes. We just amputated, we had no anaes-
thetic so I just stood there and held them whilst the doctor amputated
their hands and toes. It was awful.' It was several months before the
sailors whom Leif Andreasson had helped to save could be evacuated.
'It was bad enough when you had to step on the bodies, but it was worse
in the spring when you saw these people coming out limping and many
had lost fingers and so on, and I think that was worse than seeing the
frozen bodies.' The war went on.

The Norwegian commander, Ullring, was sure that there were
Germans further north at Neo-Alesund, the northernmost town on
Spitsbergen. In late August he sent up a party of three men to investigate. The town was empty, but when the patrol entered the North Pole
Hotel they found signs that they were not alone on the island: 'We found
in the hotel a string of grouse in the kitchen, so they'd been planning a
right feast. But *we* had that meal. It was the best meal we had during the
war . . . prunes and cream and canned fruit . . . a right feast.'

Frustrated but full, Ullring and his men returned to Longyearbyen.
There would be no more expeditions that year. But Ullring's gut instincts
were correct, for nearby at Singnehamna there was one of the longest-
running German stations in the whole war. It was a beautiful spot: on one
side there was a famous bird cliff and on the other there were two huge
glaciers. But the Germans weren't there to admire the views; this was a
vital outpost for the Navy who were willing to devote considerable time
and effort to ensure its success. It was commanded by Franz Nusser,
another veteran of peacetime exploration. He knew that in the winter
they were unlikely to be attacked: it was too dark for them to be
approached from the air and the sea was choked with ice. As soon as
spring came, security loomed much larger in everyone's thoughts. In
May they were re-supplied, when a parachute drop was made by a
Focke Wulf from Norway. A month later Nusser and two of the others
went down the mountain to check a cache of supplies which had been

left there. Suddenly they stopped in their tracks. Nusser's worst fears had come true: Ullring and his men had discovered their camp.

Ullring himself had gone back in his motor boat to get reinforcements but had left several men ashore. Nusser sent his comrades back up the hill whilst he hid behind some rocks, trying to eavesdrop on the Norwegians. After a couple of hours he too headed back, only to find that one of his team was dead. The official Norwegian report makes chilling reading:

> Heinz Kohler had descended from the mountains west of Singnehamna and was observed on his way towards the sea. When Kohler became aware of the two Norwegians about 400 yards away, he turned and fled as fast as possible with his two pursuers walking fast in the easy manner of experienced and trained hunters, gradually gaining on their prey. A few shots were fired to frighten the German whom they intended to seize alive in order to get information desired. When they were about twenty yards apart, Kohler stumbled and fell. Sitting on the ground he fired two magazines against his pursuers without hitting any. Then he turned the pistol against his head and fell down dead.

Nusser realised that he had to act quickly. He radioed Gruppe Nord in Tromsø requesting a U-boat to come and pick them up and ordered his men to retreat to an emergency camp which had been set up the previous winter. Two days later a U-boat arrived and the men scrambled aboard. The submarine cruised round the headland and back into Singnehamna. Ullring had by now returned with reinforcements and most of the Norwegians had set off to search for any remaining Germans, leaving a detachment to guard their tents. Now it was the U-boat's turn to wreak its revenge: it opened fire, destroying the motor boat and killing Harald Anderesen. Ullring and the Norwegians were stranded, but fortunately they had a radio and after seven days they were picked up by the British submarine, the *Seadog*.

The next time the Germans returned to Spitsbergen they didn't take any chances. Whether it was because they were angered by their recent setbacks, or because they overestimated the Norwegian presence on the island, or for reasons outside the Arctic campaign, *Operation*

Zitronella stands out as being one of the strangest incidents in the war. On 8 September, two German battleships and no less than ten destroyers left their base in Norway on a mission to destroy the Norwegian forces in Barentsburg and Longyearbyen. It was the only German fleet engagement in the whole of the Second World War. The *Tirpitz* was the biggest ship in the German fleet but for most of the war it hadn't even ventured out of its dock at Altafjorden in Norway. Now it was steaming northwards, on the direct orders of Hitler himself.

At 3.00 a.m. German ships were spotted by Norwegian troops stationed at Cape Heer. Before they were able to warn the garrison at Barentsburg, a deafening bombardment began. For almost three and a half hours, the German ships rained shell after shell on to the town. The garrison fought back bravely and managed to score at least one direct hit on a destroyer, but they were outgunned and outnumbered. When there was little left but burning rubble, the Germans landed shore parties to finish off the destruction and mop up any resistance.

The attack on Longyearbyen was just as devastating and even more cowardly. Leif Andreasson was in charge of an anti-aircraft battery at the edge of the town when the first ships arrived.

> *We saw a ship coming flying a British flag, and suddenly I saw an aeroplane so I thought that they were going to attack the British ship coming in. I swung my gun up in the air to shoot at it, but we heard it go away so there must have been some connection between the ship and the plane. Then we saw that they had lowered the British flag and they opened fire. It was hell – I hadn't been in that sort of attack before but you have to move fast, I'm telling you.*

Again, the German gunners blanketed the town with shells before landing shore parties. The Norwegians were forced to retreat further and further up the valley until they reached a group of buildings which were out of sight of the naval guns. As a final act of wanton destruction, German ground troops blew up Longyearbyen's famous church. At 11.30 the sirens blared out and the troops returned to their ships. In barely six and a half hours most of Spitsbergen had been laid waste. The Norwegians had suffered a serious setback – six men killed and forty-one taken prisoner – but they were undeterred. On 19 October two US ships and three British destroyers arrived with reinforcements and before the winter set in a new weather station was built. For the German newsreels this was a heroic battle but the return of the German fleet to the high seas was short-lived. The *Scharnhorst* was sunk off North Cape in December and the *Tirpitz* was pinned down by persistent attacks for a whole year until November 1944, when it too was sunk. Today the veterans of the attack look back on the events with bemusement as well as bitterness:

It was a morale thing, to allow the German sailors to get their kicks, so they could get more spirit. They had never been out, they had just been sneaking along the Norwegian coast. We heard afterwards how they made a lot of propaganda out of it, over how many Russians they had killed – but that of course was bullshit.

As early as 1939, German scientists had begun a research programme to develop automatic weather stations which could be put in position by submarines and left to transmit by themselves. The first of these was deployed in September 1942, but as the war went on, numbers grew. They were ingenious machines which could gather weather information for up to six months and work at temperatures as low as -40°C. Automatic stations were set up in both Greenland and Spitsbergen and one was even placed on the shores of Labrador on the North American mainland. It wasn't found until 1981 when it was finally picked up: rusty, damaged but still intact. The unmanned programme was remarkably successful but it had its limitations, and right until the end of the war the German military continued to place a high priority on sending well-equipped expeditions to the Arctic – though Allied harassment forced them to look for ever more remote sites.

The last operation to take place on Svalbard was code-named *Haudegen* and led by Wilhelm Dege, a schoolteacher who had been to Spitsbergen several times in the late thirties. It cost one and a half million marks to outfit the weather station and Dege was given a free hand to choose whoever he wanted for the expedition. He set off in an armoured trawler for Rijpfjorden, Nordaustlandet, a large island just north of Spitsbergen in September 1944 with a party of eleven men, eighty tonnes of supplies and enough ammunition and explosives to defend themselves against a small army. Dege chose Rijpfjorden because he knew that there was enough game in the area and enough driftwood available to sustain his team if they had to stay there longer than anticipated. He assumed that ice would keep sea-based attacks at bay for most of the year, but he was worried about a land-based assault and took the precaution of destroying any nearby trappers' huts in case these could be used during an enemy operation. He also sent a team to look for the base camp of the Oxford University expedition of 1937, but they never managed to find it.

By October most of the station had been constructed and the men prepared for the Arctic night. Like all good leaders, Dege knew that half the battle would be to keep his men's morale up. He set up classes in everything from mathematics to the history of polar exploration. Everyone had been allowed to take along a musical instrument to keep them amused, but Dege opted for a movie-camera instead and set about filming the boisterous efforts of the 'North Pole Band'. He waited until 1 December to begin transmitting weather information, by which time he felt that an attack was extremely unlikely, but his men did have to contend with marauding polar bears and ferocious blizzards which could turn the fifteen-metre walk between their bunkhouse and the observation hut into a life-threatening expedition. On Christmas Eve 1944 they unpacked their presents and sat down to a huge Christmas dinner: reindeer, asparagus, tinned apricots and cognac. Dege even invented a special 'Northern Lights' cocktail to unbatten the hatches.

On 23 February 1945 everyone was thrilled to see the sun rise for the first time in four months, but the news of the war from Germany tempered their joy. Allied forces had begun to break in to their transmission frequency and their threat was clear: 'We'll get you swine yet.' Dege received news from Germany that the naval authorities were considering leaving his party on Nordaustlandet for another year. At the end of April they were told to get ready for the arrival of a re-supply plane but it never came. Then on 7 May they heard that Germany had surrendered. Dege burnt his code books, ordered the removal of the camouflage netting and began transmitting unencrypted weather information.

Over the next four months he took the opportunity to make several journeys around Nordaustlandet, much of which was still relatively unexplored and unmapped. Clearly Dege was pleased to have the opportunity to continue his scientific work in the Arctic and though his men were desperate for news of their families, no one was looking forward to the future in a prisoner-of-war camp.

In mid-July they were asked for their exact position by the Norwegian meteorological service and then ordered to go down to Longyearbyen to surrender. But they weren't given any further information and so Dege did nothing. A month later, when the bay began to fill up with ice, Dege sent an urgent message to Oslo warning that the supplies which they had been asked to surrender would be damaged by bad weather if they weren't picked up soon. Finally, on 3 September 1945, a Norwegian sealer, the *Blaasel*, arrived flying an enormous naval flag. After some initial hesitation, Dege and his men were greeted warmly by men who regarded them not as enemies but as fellow northerners. Years later, Wilhelm Dege told his son Eckart the strange story of that final day:

> Round midnight the Norwegian captain got a bit nervous and
> he said that the authorities had told him that the Germans
> should surrender. The only trouble was that he didn't know
> what to do. My father said that he didn't know what to do either
> and so these two men sat around the table and they wrote a
> contract and both men signed it and my father gave his pistol to
> the captain. The captain asked a little nervously 'Can I keep it?'
> and my father said 'Of course' and so this was the last surrender
> of a German military unit of the Second World War.

As the *Blaasel* sailed out of Rijpfjorden Dege tossed his cap into the receding waves and turned to his men: 'You may remember this as the hardest year of your life, but in the future you'll also remember it as the best year.' When they returned to Norway the men were interrogated before being shipped back to Germany where they were demobilised. Four of them, whose homes were in East Germany, were allowed to stay and work on mine-sweepers on the Norwegian coast.

The 'War for the Weather' may be regarded as a footnote in the history of the Second World War, but for the Arctic it heralded a new phase in its 'conquest'; within a few years it would become one of the main theatres for the Cold War. For both sides, the Arctic itself was the the main antagonist. The weather determined the time of year in which events took place and could reek havoc with the best laid plans. For the men who fought in the Arctic it was an unusual conflict, but then they were unusual men. Few of them had any military background and many of them had friends on the other side. There was a certain amount of gentlemanly conduct on both sides, but though casualties were small they were no less cruel. Toralf Lund lost his father and his brother on board the *Isbjorn* in 1942, and for years Atle Gresli could not even talk to his wife about the horrific attack. Today though, he and the dwindling band of veterans keep in close contact, sharing their unforgettable memories:

> It was very strange. It was the only time in my life that I felt really alive! Those months there on Spitsbergen. Because we were living from day to day with all our senses totally alive. It was a strange feeling, being really alive.

Chapter Nine

OVER AND UNDER

Only two days after the end of the war in Europe, a specially adapted RAF Lancaster, her bomb load replaced by extra fuel tanks, took off from Iceland for a reconnaissance flight over the North Pole. *Aries 1* was the first in a systematic programme of flights across Arctic territory conducted by the RAF. Their purpose was to obtain meteorological data, and to study conditions for aerial navigation, but what lay behind the programme was the recognition among wartime military strategists that the map of the world was changing.

During the war, weather stations operated from the northernmost Arctic land masses, convoys between Britain and Russia sailed as far north as they dared, and air-bases were built in the inhospitable terrain of west Greenland as part of an aerial supply route from America to Europe, close to the Arctic Circle. Only the southerly fringes of the Arctic were dragged into the war. The vast wilderness of the frozen Polar Sea was undisturbed, but it was not destined to remain so. When the tide turned against Hitler and a new world order began to evolve, it became clear that soon after Germany surrendered the strategists in the war rooms of Washington, London and Moscow would need to start using an unfamiliar projection of the world map. The emergence of two super-powers was giving the Arctic, the shortest aerial route between them, the appearance of a frontier zone. It was no longer useful to think of the Arctic Ocean as the top of the world, but as its centre, a frozen mediter-ranean sea enclosed in the east by the long coast of the Soviet Union, and bordered in the west by the top of the North American continent. Shortly after the outbreak of peace the American General H. H. Arnold predicted: 'If World War III should come, its strategic centre will be the North Pole.'

The RAF may have been first off the mark, but in 1946 the

Americans began a more ambitious – and secret – programme of polar flying. Using B-29 Superfortresses, the long-range aircraft that had carried the atomic bombs to Hiroshima and Nagasaki, the USAF concentrated on areas within the Arctic Ocean that had not previously been explored. The intensive programme, operating from Alaska, was described officially as weather reconnaissance, but one of its undisclosed objectives was to search for any undiscovered land masses within the Arctic basin, and to find them before the Soviets. More than a million photographs were taken. According to one of the USAF officers:

If we found land and could claim it on behalf of the United
States, we could get forward bases closer to the Soviet Union,
instead of way back in Alaska and into Canada.

By 1951 the Americans were making almost daily flights over the North Pole and the Barents Sea. No land was ever found, but a series of remarkable 'ice islands' were discovered. The first, christened T1, was spotted 300 miles north of Point Barrow, Alaska. It measured seventeen miles by eight and was initially mistaken for land: patches of earth, gravel and small lakes could be seen on its surface. However, subsequent reconnaissance flights found that its position had changed, and the USAF concluded that it was a colossal fragment of ice that had probably broken away from a glacier on Ellesmere Island. Two further ice islands were discovered. T3, nine miles by four, was later used as the base for a weather station and 'listening post' – to monitor Soviet activity. It became known as Fletcher Island, after the USAF Colonel who led the operation to land on the 'natural aircraft carrier' and establish the station. During his time there, in the spring of 1952, Joe Fletcher flew the one hundred miles from T3 in order to make the first landing by an aeroplane at the Pole. If the consensus against Robert Peary's claim is correct, then Fletcher is the first man to have stood at the North Pole. He now lives in Colorado, and has no interest in claiming the distinction.

The discovery of the ice islands intrigued students of Arctic history. Peary believed he had seen land through his binoculars from the north of Ellesmere Island in 1906 and named it after one of his backers. Subsequent expeditions in search of 'Croker Land', however, had found nothing. Some commentators believed Peary was deceived by an optical illusion, while detractors pointed to his record of exaggeration and, arguably, of invention. Was it possible that Peary saw an ice island? The islands are now known to drift around the Arctic Ocean for many hundreds of miles. Frederick Cook's supporters use this argument to account for 'Bradley Land', which he claimed to have seen en route to the Pole.

On 3 September 1949, one of the B-29 Superfortresses of the Weather Reconnaissance Squadron operating from Alaska returned to its base with information that would send shock waves through America. The aircraft was fitted with a device for the detection of radioactive debris, and abnormally high levels had been recorded in a flight near the Kamchatka Peninsula in the eastern Soviet Union. Although monitoring of radiation levels had begun, the Americans believed that their Soviet counterparts were at least three years away from detonating their first atomic bomb. However, the quantity of radioactive dust on the aircraft's filter papers pointed unmistakably to an atomic explosion some four days earlier at the Soviet testing ground, the vast Arctic island of Novaya Zemlya. President Truman made the grim announcement to the nation on 23 September.

When, a short time later, it emerged that the Soviet Union had developed a bomber aircraft capable of flying the 4000 miles over the Arctic and delivering its payload to American cities, an unfamiliar feeling of acute vulnerability swept across the nation. The Soviet Tu-4 bomber was a copy of the American Superfortress. Its range would not have permitted its pilot and crew to make the return flight to the Soviet Union, but the threat of one-way missions seemed entirely plausible to both the American public and the defence establishment – although a report conceded that 'this tactic would have obvious limitations'. Planners were in no doubt that the development of longer-range bombers, refuelling in-flight, was only a matter of time.

Radar defences existed, but the public knew they were too close to the heartland of the United States to provide adequate warning of an attack. At the northern limit of the continent, from where attacks were bound to come, there was nothing. The government responded swiftly by commissioning a series of research projects on national defence which culminated in the setting up of a special laboratory at the Massachusetts Institute of Technology in the summer of 1952. The so-called 'Summer Study Group' of scientists, engineers and military personnel concluded that current defence systems could be 'surprised, saturated, and avoided' by a low-altitude transpolar attack. Soviet atomic bombs, it estimated, could 'destroy or injure' up to forty million Americans (the figure was calculated on the basis of 'roughly, one megadeath per megaton'). The group proposed 'measures of a kind and on a scale not hitherto considered in defence planning': the construction of a line of radar stations across the entire 3000-mile breadth of the North American Arctic, from Alaska to Greenland. At this latitude, the Distant Early Warning – or DEW Line – would provide between three and six hours' notice of an attack from the north.

'Project 572' was authorised in December 1952. By the autumn of 1953 an experimental section of the line had been built in Alaska and was proved to work. With the co-operation of the Dominion of Canada, construction now began on sites reaching from Alaska to Baffin Island. One of the largest engineering projects ever undertaken, its location included some of the most inhospitable territories on the globe. Six main radar sites divided the DEW Line into 500-mile sectors. Within these, auxiliary sites were built at 100-mile intervals, while much smaller inter-mediate stations were placed wherever a gap in the line was apparent. Mapping teams travelled over a million miles to locate suitable positions for nearly fifty installations, taking over 80,000 aerial photographs. Construction materials were shipped in convoys of up to 120 vessels, including 46,000 tons of steel and such a vast quantity of gravel that it would have been sufficient to build a road eighteen feet wide and one foot thick from Florida to California. More than 20,000 workers were engaged. Airstrips built at the sites covered 625 acres, and over 45,000 commercial flights were made to bring in supplies – sixty of them crashed. American citizens nervous about their northern frontier were soothed by the flow of spectacular statistics.

Before the early-warning line took shape, the Americans began the construction of a vast Arctic air-base, intended as the springboard for a retaliatory attack across the Polar Sea. The site chosen was Thule in west Greenland, a short distance south of the fjord from which Robert Peary had made his first crossing of the Greenland ice cap in 1892. At 75° N, it was only 930 miles from the Pole and 500 miles north of the DEW Line. Sixty years before, when Peary's party had wintered in a wooden hut, they were entirely cut off from the civilised world. Few of the Eskimos they met had ever seen a white man – or a black man. In 1951 the Thule Eskimos, including descendants of Peary and Henson, were moved sixty miles north by the Danish authorities in order to make way for the great American base. By the mid-1950s, 6000 personnel were stationed there and a 10,000-foot runway had been built on the permafrost. When the summer sun beat down on it, the American engineers discovered that the bitumen absorbed the heat, melted the permafrost and flooded nearby installations. Their solution was to spray the runway with 17,000 gallons of white paint.

At Thule and at the DEW Line stations, each problem presented by a uniquely hostile environment was overcome either by the ingenuity of engineers or by a massive commitment of men, materials and money. In the most difficult locations for the radar installations, the initial party of engineers landed by helicopter, while tractors were dropped by parachute. A new kind of radio communication was devised in order to avoid magnetic disturbances and the effects of frequent, violent storms. The name alone – Forward Propagation Tropospheric Scatter – is enough to suggest that high technology had arrived in the wilderness. To protect the radars from winds of over 100 m.p.h., they were housed in eye-catching spheres comprised of hundreds of interlocking triangles. The design was based on the 'geodesic domes' of the architect Buckminster Fuller. No expense was spared on the comfort of men operating the stations. At Thule there was a multi-denominational chapel, a resident professor, a gymnasium and workshops for those interested in carpentry, pottery and photography. On the DEW Line food was so plentiful that men beginning a tour of duty were advised to bring clothes a size bigger than they were used to.

In the space of a few years the construction programmes permanently changed the North American Arctic. Commercial airlines operated along the DEW Line and communications were established from one side of the continent to the other. The *National Geographic Magazine* of 1957 observed:

You may now fly completely across the North American Arctic without losing sight of the lights of a human habitation, and rarely being more than twenty-five miles from an airstrip.

Eskimos were given work on many of the sites, and small settlements grew up around the larger bases. For many of them the traditional way of life disappeared altogether, and it has often been said that since the beginning of the Cold War they have moved directly from the Stone Age into the Space Age.

By the time the DEW Line was completed, on schedule, in the summer of 1957, at a cost of more than $600,000,000, it was already on the verge of obsolescence. The long-range bomber remained the principal weapon of each side, but military planners knew that within a few years – as soon as the technology had been perfected – aircraft would begin to give way to intercontinental ballistic missiles. They were faster and cheaper and, as far as the DEW Line was concerned, invisible.

As early as 1956 a new radar system was under construction at Thule air-base. At the new Ballistic Missile Early Warning Site (BMEWS) four radar antennae rose into the Arctic sky, each as big as a football pitch. They could detect a missile on the other side of the North Pole, 3000 miles away: at the rate the missiles travelled, BMEWS would be able to furnish the United States with between fifteen and thirty minutes' warning of an impending attack. A defensive crescent was formed with two other missile radars – at Clear, Alaska, and Fylingdales, Yorkshire. From 1960 American strategic bombers were put on twenty-four-hour 'airborne alert': at any given time some aircraft, armed with atomic weapons, would be in the air. It provided a 'credible retaliatory capability', in spite of the short warning period from the radars. While giant bombers patrolled the Arctic skies, American army scientists considered further means of defending their northern frontier.

On the Greenland ice cap, more than a hundred miles from Thule, the tip of a communication mast that was once 200 feet high is the only trace of an experimental military installation built *under the ice*. Camp Century was the brainchild of the US Army Polar Research and Development Center. In 1960 a visitor to the site would have seen nothing on the monotonous expanse of the ice cap except the towering mast and, apparently, fifteen small chimneys protruding a few feet above the surface. They were, in fact, escape hatches. At the foot of the ladders there was a miniature atomic city of over a hundred soldiers and scientists. Wayne Tobiasson was one of the latter:

> The idea behind Century was to test whether or not people
> could fight and live out on the Greenland ice cap. It was a very
> inhospitable place, and any time you want to build something
> or maintain a hundred troops in a remote area it's really a lesson

in logistics. So Camp Century was a trial of the constructability
of a different kind of installation, in case the remote chance
happened that we had to go out there and do something due to
a confrontation with the Soviets.

In an uncertain future Greenland might become the location for missile-launching sites or ground-to-air batteries to defend the air-base at Thule, but in 1960 the emphasis of the Century experiment was on finding the best way to survive there. By building under the ice, the military planners hoped to discover an advantage over surface structures which, high up on the ice cap, would be battered by fierce gales, drifting snow and intense cold. Atomic power provided long-term independence for the secret city. The main street was a tunnel 1100 feet long, to which twenty-one further tunnels were connected. They contained prefabricated accommodation for the men, a mess hall and kitchen with a serving capacity of 200, shower rooms and latrines, a communication centre and a portable nuclear reactor. There was no landing strip. All the materials and equipment for its construction arrived in twenty-ton sledge wagons pulled in long trains by giant tractors – each caterpillar track was wider than the wheelbase of a jeep. They moved at walking pace, and the journey from Thule took several days. 'You felt like a pioneer in an old wagon heading out to the west,' says Tobiasson.

Scientists conducted a series of experiments to learn what they could about their new environment. Drilling 4500 feet to the rock at the bottom of the ice cap, they retrieved fragments of ice that had fallen as snow many thousands of years before. Their impacted layers, like the rings in a tree, could accurately date the 'ice cores'; they provided valuable data about the inexorable movement of the cap and the pattern of climatic changes.

If it was an exciting opportunity for scientists, the soldiers stationed at Century were less enthusiastic. 'If you suffer from claustrophobia,' says Herb Ueda, 'it wasn't the place for you, especially in some of the smaller, tighter tunnels.' He likened the station to 'a ship out in the middle of a frozen sea', and their long isolation caused problems of morale just as it had in the era of Parry, Ross and Franklin. Tobiasson recalls an attempted escape:

One Friday night a fellow just left a note on the First Sergeant's desk saying, 'Sorry, Sarge, I just can't take it any more. I'm heading home.' He hopped into a tractor, which could do at most three or four miles per hour, and headed down the trail. He finally fell asleep at the wheel, maybe halfway to the air-base. On Monday they found his note. He was pretty cold when the helicopters picked him up.

Entertainment was scarce. When a scientist obtained a grant from an army agency to study the effect of the cold on the healing of injuries, there was a welcome diversion from the monotony of their work:

He brought a whole bunch of rabbits up to Camp Century. Some of the rabbits were kept nice and warm and others were put out in the cold. He was opening up wounds in the rabbits and sewing them up. They had little inflatable things inside the wounds so that after a day or a week or whatever they could then determine the bursting pressure of the wound. There were a lot of stories that went around about those rabbits that year . . . it gave us something else to talk about.

There were unforeseen problems for Camp Century. Snow accumulated on the surface at a rate of nearly three feet a year, gradually increasing the weight on the roofs of the tunnels. A combination of growing pressure and the effect of heat inside Camp Century caused the walls and ceilings of ice to close in much more quickly than they expected. Once a year, fifty-strong teams of chainsaw operators shaved the encroaching ice from the inside of the tunnels, but the installation was doomed, and by the mid-1960s it had been abandoned. The remains of Century are now thought to be about a hundred feet below the surface of the ice cap. Eventually, the tip of the radio mast will disappear.

Camp Century may have been a failure, but the future of the Cold War lay under the ice, and with atomic power. The nuclear submarine was the vehicle the Arctic had been waiting for. The advantages of travelling under rather than over the ice of the Arctic Ocean had been discussed ever since Simon Lake developed the first practical submarine in 1897. The *Argonaut* rolled along the seabed on wheels. In 1931, the concept was inverted for the first attempt to reach the North Pole in a submarine – by sledging along the *underneath* of the pack ice.

The *Nautilus* expedition of 1931 was the work of the Australian-born explorer, Sir George Hubert Wilkins. He was used to scepticism. In 1928 he made the first crossing of the Arctic basin in an aeroplane, a feat Amundsen had warned him was 'beyond the possibility of human endeavour'. Had the Norwegian lived to hear about Wilkins' plans for the *Nautilus*, he might have been lost for words. The simple verdict of many commentators was that the expedition was 'suicide'.

In a decommissioned First World War submarine that he bought for the nominal fee of one dollar, Wilkins intended to penetrate the ice-pack north of Spitsbergen and, when there was no more open water, slide underneath the ice by means of inverted runners fitted along its deck. In case of collision with underwater pressure ridges, an hydraulic cushioning bumper extended from the nose of the ship. The *Nautilus* could remain submerged for a maximum of sixteen hours before it became necessary to replenish the air and run the diesel engines in order to recharge the batteries. If they could not find an open lead or a polynya – a small lake – in which to surface, a special drill would bore a hole through the ice and suck in the air. 'Men drill thousands of feet *down* to get oil,' he reasoned, 'surely we can drill a mere fifteen feet *up*.'

Renamed after the fictional submarine in Jules Verne's *Twenty Thousand Leagues Under the Sea* and christened in the presence of the author's grandson, the *Nautilus* sailed from New York in the summer of 1931 in a circus of publicity. To raise money during the fitting out of the submarine, Wilkins had taken the unusual step of publishing a book about the expedition in advance of its departure. It was as well that he had, in the opinion of sceptical readers, since he might not live to write a retrospective account.

Despite a series of mechanical problems during the crossing of the Atlantic, Wilkins was undaunted. The *Nautilus* was repaired in Plymouth, and made her way via Bergen to Tromsø. It was in Norway that some members of the crew suddenly lost confidence in the enterprise. They considered the unreliability of the submarine, contemplated the risk of a horrible death from suffocation, observed the serene optimism of their expedition leader, and decided to take matters into their own hands. Using a hacksaw, they removed the diving rudders.

It was not until they approached the pack ice north of Spitsbergen and attempted their first dive that the sabotage was discovered. Without the rudders, it was impossible to control the *Nautilus* under water, and the planned voyage under the ice to the North Pole had to be abandoned. Wilkins was nevertheless determined to take the submarine as far north as possible through the broken ice at the edge of the pack, and to experiment with the technique of sliding under an ice-floe on her inverted runners. By reaching eighty-two degrees of latitude, a hundred miles beyond Spitsbergen, the *Nautilus* set a northerly record for a ship moving under her own power. Several attempts were made to slide under the ice by ramming a floe, but on each occasion the *Nautilus* stalled with only her bow submerged, her propellers spinning in the air. The submarine captain dared not reduce her buoyancy and eventually Wilkins conceded defeat. Through the portholes in the bow of the submarine he had filmed the underside of the ice-floe. 'No human eyes had ever before looked on this sight,' he wrote, and in spite of the failure of his expedition he was certain that there would be successors:

> There was no doubt in my mind that ours was but the first of a great submarine fleet that would one day cruise at will beneath the Arctic ice cap, the shortest distance between the great American and Eurasian land masses.

Wilkins envisaged a submarine trade route operating in a time of peace. The advent of nuclear powered submarines made his dream possible, but the demands of the Cold War, rather than commerce, turned it into a reality.

In the summer of 1958 a very different *Nautilus* became the first submarine to traverse the Arctic basin and pass underneath the North Pole. The USS *Nautilus* was the American Navy's first nuclear submarine and, in the sense that it could operate in almost complete independence from the surface, the first true submarine ever built. She could remain submerged for up to two months. For navigation under a canopy of Arctic ice she was the perfect machine.

The American Navy had a good reason for sending the *Nautilus*, and her sister ship the *Skate*, to the Polar Sea. By the late 1950s, a race was under way to design a nuclear submarine that could fire missiles. Admiral James Calvert, the former commander of the *Skate*, recalls:

> Ours were still in the developmental stage, and we didn't know whether the Russians had them or not. It turns out that they

*were developing them. A submarine that could go up to the
Arctic, surface in a polynya, probably stay there undetected for
two or three days until it had its position absolutely firm, and
fire missiles into the United States was a very dangerous thing
because all of our defences against the Russian missiles in those
days were based on the assumption that they came from certain
directions.*

If the military significance of the voyage of the *Nautilus* was unclear to the American public, its propaganda value was obvious to defence chiefs. The Soviet Union had recently pulled off a spectacular coup by launching the first orbiting satellite, or *sputnik*, and the Pentagon had an urgent need to demonstrate its own potency. The *Nautilus* was chosen ahead of the *Skate* to make the first transit under the Pole because she was considered to have a more sexy name than her sister ship; as soon as the feat was accomplished she was sent on a triumphant tour of European and American ports.

A more important task fell to James Calvert's ship: to demonstrate that a submarine could locate openings in the pack ice from beneath and rise into them. A few days after the voyage of the *Nautilus*, the *Skate* moved under the permanent sea ice north of Spitsbergen and surfaced nine times in polynyas and leads.

When he returned to Boston at the end of the summer, Calvert received a visit on board the *Skate* from Sir Hubert Wilkins. Twentyseven years had passed since his pioneer voyage. From what Calvert knew of Wilkins' expedition, he was convinced that the act of sabotage by his crew had saved the explorer's life: he had no means of detecting open water other than by luck. 'I felt a little ashamed,' Calvert said, 'telling him about the wealth of mechanical devices we possessed.' Wilkins urged him to take the *Skate* to the Arctic in winter-time, when open water is scarce, and experiment with drilling a hole through the ice or blasting it away with explosives. Six weeks later, Calvert learned that the old man had died of a heart attack.

The American Navy was indeed planning to send the *Skate* north before the end of the winter. They needed to know if she could accurately determine the thickness of the ice above and, where it was relatively thin, push through without damaging the submarine. The *Skate*'s conning tower was specially strengthened for the purpose. If conditions were favourable Calvert would attempt to pull off another propaganda victory by bringing his ship to the surface at the North Pole itself.

Before they sailed Calvert paid a visit to Lady Wilkins in New York:

She was a little different than other people. I mean she dressed in a rather extravagant way, the art in her apartment was unusual, the apartment itself was unusual. Lady Wilkins was a person that we might think of as – I can't think of a respectful word, but maybe 'flaky'.

She had an unusual request: that Calvert should take the bronze urn containing her husband's ashes and scatter them at the North Pole. Calvert agreed, but was concerned that the *Skate* might be unable to surface in the right place. A colleague suggested shooting the ashes out of a torpedo tube, but Calvert told him that Wilkins 'wouldn't have wanted it that way'. He took the urn with him and hoped for the best when the *Skate* sailed on 3 March.

Two weeks later, the *Skate* arrived under the Pole and began looking for areas of thin ice – newly frozen leads. They called them skylights: 'they were like a stretch of blue-green translucent glass in an otherwise black ceiling.' When one was found within a hundred yards of what they calculated to be the exact position of the North Pole, Calvert gave the order to surface, the periscope was lowered and the men braced themselves for a collision. The ship shuddered, lurched and broke through.

It was 17 March, two days before the rising of the sun, and the darkness was almost complete. The broken ice around the conning tower was nearly three feet thick. Dark clouds gathered and a freezing wind turned their breath to ice. 'It wasn't the kind of place,' Calvert said, 'you would like to go on a picnic'. He did not plan to be there long.

A small table was carried on to the ice, and the urn containing Wilkins' ashes placed upon it. Seven men held burning flares while Calvert read a prayer.

The flares made a sort of ghostly red light around. We formed a semicircle. I read the burial at sea service from the Episcopal Book of Common Prayer, and we got to the place where it was time to do it – there was quite a strong wind blowing and one of

*the men just threw the ashes up in the air and they scattered
and at that point I read the 'sure and certain hope of
resurrection'. I think all of us felt it would have been nice to
have had some music with it.*

The strange memorial service for Sir Hubert Wilkins invoked memories
of an heroic period of Arctic exploration that had long since passed.
Now that a submarine could surface at the North Pole, anything was
possible in the Arctic. During the next thirty years submarines of the
American and Soviet navies made hundreds of voyages beneath the
polar ice cap and accumulated a vast quantity of information about
every aspect of the Arctic from the seasonal movement of the ice to the
topography of the ocean floor. The billions of dollars invested by both
governments reflected the rising importance of the Arctic as a theatre of
the Cold War. As ballistic missile submarines became more sophisticated, they played an increasingly important role in the superpowers'
nuclear armouries. The Arctic was the ideal place to hide them. Invisible
from the air and difficult to detect when submerged amidst the ambient
noise of the pack ice, a submarine operating in the dark waters of the
Arctic Ocean was almost invulnerable to attack.

With its long northern coastline, the Soviet Union placed special
emphasis on deploying its missile submarines in the Arctic, while the
Americans in turn sent their hunter-killer submarines under the ice to
practise flushing them out. During the Reagan period of 'aggressive
defence', the game of cat and mouse threatened to turn nasty. 'The
battle for the North Pole has started,' declared the American Chief of
Naval Operations in 1983. 'It is a covert war, with fish the only witnesses.' If it started, it was never finished. The competition for military
supremacy under the polar ice was interrupted by the sound of the
Berlin Wall coming down.

In 1997 the Cold War is over, and many of the submarines of the
Russian northern fleet are rusting in the docks of the Kola Peninsula.
Much of the invaluable data collected by the submarines and meteorological stations of both sides since the Second World War is being
declassified, and made available to scientists studying the last mystery
of the Arctic: what it can tell us about the ecology of our planet.

Thule air-base is still operational. The DEW Line began to shrink in
the mid-1960s, but many installations were retained as part of the North

Warning System developed during the Reagan era. One of the surviving DEW Line sites is at Hall Beach on Baffin Island. The original antennae, more than a hundred feet high, are no longer in use, but some of the local Eskimos protested at the suggestion that they should be pulled down: they were accustomed to using them as a landmark on their hunting trips.

Chapter 10

A TOWN CALLED RESOLUTE

'Cornwallis Island is perhaps one of the most dreary and desolate spots that can well be conceived.'

Papers of HMS *Assistance*, 1854, and
Page one of Resolute tourist guide, 1997

On 7 September 1953, in the midst of a snowstorm, a small boat drew up to the shores of Resolute Bay, Cornwallis Island, and deposited nineteen Inuit and a lone representative of the Royal Canadian Mounted Police. The new arrivals took a quick look at the harsh gravel beach and then immediately set to work erecting the tents which they had taken with them from their homes in Port Harrison in Quebec, over 1000 miles away. For the RCMP and government officials back in Ottawa, this was the start of a pioneer experiment to see if they could colonise and 'Canadianise' the remote islands of the High Arctic. For the Inuit it was the beginning of a long exile from their homelands and an experience which would leave them bitter and disillusioned. In years to come they would claim that they had been treated like pawns in a complex Cold War chess game, sent north to bolster Canada's territorial claims in the face of increased American activity in the Arctic. It took forty years for their story to come to light but when the Inuit finally faced the cameras in 1993 the whole nation shivered.

Today most Canadians call them by their own name for themselves – 'Inuit' meaning 'the people' – but for centuries they were known as 'Eskimos' from the French *Esquimaux* or 'eaters of raw flesh'. Their most common name for whites is *kabloona* or 'pale face'; other Inuit expressions include *Arnasiutiit,* 'stealers of our women'. The white explorers who first encountered the Inuit looked upon them with a mixture of curiosity and condescension. In the early nineteenth century Sir John Barrow was content to send off expedition after expedition in search of the Northwest Passage but he couldn't for the life of him work out why the Inuit put up with their 'cruel and wretched lot' and wondered if perhaps 'persecution could have driven them to take up their abode in these extreme parts of the globe'. Amundsen, Cook and Peary all took Eskimos back to Europe and America where they were shown off to eager spectators. Leaving aside Dickens' attack on the Eskimos for their 'domesticity of blood and blubber', in general the Eskimos enjoyed a good press. They were regarded as infinitely more noble than the southern hemisphere's 'savages'.

In the middle of the nineteenth century whaling ships came from Europe and the United States and set up stations in the eastern Arctic. They employed the Inuit as boat pilots and manual labourers and periodically moved them around the archipelago if they needed to set up camp in a different area. There was a lot of fraternisation with Inuit women and the whalers were quite happy to give them alcohol, even encouraging them to distil their own. By 1910 most of the whales had been killed and so the whalers abandoned the Arctic. In their place came clergymen and traders, dedicated to saving Inuit souls and making as much money as possible out of them.

The Inuit had always lived a precarious existence. The were essentially nomadic hunters for whom trade only played a small part in their economy. In times of plenty they prospered, but if for some reason the caribou migration was late one year or the seals were struck by disease, then they starved. Their oral history is full of tales of famines and horrific stories of families having to resort to cannibalism in dire necessity. By the late nineteenth century the lives of most Inuit had been irrevocably changed. The white traders gradually turned the Inuit into trappers rather than hunters. 'Country food' which they hunted themselves remained a crucial part of the Inuit diet, but they became increasingly dependent on the provisions which they purchased at white trading posts in return for furs. When in the 1940s the bottom fell out of the fur market and the number of caribou in the eastern Arctic reached an all-time low, the Inuit faced total disaster – an event for which the Canadian government was almost totally unprepared.

Unlike the United States and Denmark, for most of the century Canada had been content to maintain a hands-off approach to its territory and its citizens in the Arctic. In the famous words of the Canadian prime minister, Louis St Laurent, they were governed 'in an almost continual state of absent-mindedness for ninety years'. In the forties the Inuit were given metal dog-tags and Eskimo identity numbers and included in the Canadian census for the first time. In 1951 the government counted 9493 Inuit in Canada and noted that most of them still lived a semi-nomadic existence. A year later they were front-page news.

It was Farley Mowat's controversial and highly successful book *The People of the Deer* which gave the mandarins back in Ottawa such a rude awakening. Here was a harrowing tale of the starvation and suffering experienced by the natives of Manitoba:

They are a passive, beaten, hopeless people who wait miserably for death. They are unclean, weak-bodied, sick caricatures of men, who spend their days in an apathy broken only when utter necessity drives them to make an effort to live a little longer.

Mowat argued passionately that the current state of the Inuit was a direct result of the actions of the white traders and demanded that something should be done. Though many of the Canadian civil servants claimed that Mowat was prone to wild exaggeration, the government was severely embarrassed by the international attention which the book received. They decided that now they had a bona fide 'Eskimo Problem' and a conference was called for in Ottawa in May to work out what to do about it. Needless to say, no Inuit were invited to attend.

Most of the government officials agreed that the current crisis was caused by the seemingly inexorable decline in the caribou population which had puzzled biologists for many years. Coupled with the collapse in the fur market this had driven some Inuit towards starvation and others to become increasingly dependent on government relief. In 1949 furs were worth six times less than they had been ten years earlier whilst food prices had trebled because of inflation. Family allowance and government relief had been introduced in 1944 and by the early fifties the social security bill for the Arctic was enormous. Many officials believed there was a danger of the Inuit succumbing to a 'dependency culture'. Whilst the image of the independent 'noble Eskimo' persisted, there were those who regarded the Inuit as natural opportunists and warned that they would take the easy option and become a class of 'Arctic bums' surviving on government hand-outs, loitering around Arctic shanty-towns.

One proposal which appeared in a report entitled *The Future of the Canadian Eskimo* advocated resettling the Inuit in three settlements in the south, a solution which had the advantage of making it easier to offer cultural benefits to a civilisation 'without hope of advancement' which 'should be ruthlessly discouraged'. It was envisaged that within two or three generations the Inuit would become skilled workers: 'there could be 1000 Eskimo women at least making sausage cases in our packing plants alongside the new Canadians who do this job now. In this sort of program there is a future.' Such a radical solution had few supporters, but the idea of moving the Inuit around the Arctic did take hold.

Officials at the newly formed Department of Indian Affairs and Northern Development came up with an 'experimental' project to transfer Inuit from what they perceived to be the overpopulated areas of north Quebec up to the remote and uninhabited islands of the High Arctic which they believed would be able to sustain a number of small colonies. In spite of the fact that when this process had been tried out in the past by the Hudson's Bay Company it had rarely been successful, the officials in Ottawa and the Royal Canadian Mounted Police officers who were in more direct contact with the Inuit claimed that this would be in the best interests of the Inuit. They hoped that the men and women chosen for relocation would regain their former independence in what they termed a 'rehabilitation project'.

And so in the spring of 1953 officers of the RCMP in Port Harrison in northern Quebec made a number of calls at Inuit camps hoping to find 'volunteers' to take north. Large numbers of Inuit had lived in the Port Harrison area for many years and it was one of biggest white settlements in the Arctic; there had been an RCMP post here since 1935, there was a Hudson's Bay Company post, a church, a nursing station and a small school. It also had one of the largest social security bills in the whole of the region and the natives were deemed suitable for 'rehabilitation', though nobody told them that. The support of the police was crucial to the department's plan: they would have to open up posts and administer the new settlements. Their role in the selection of the Inuit would later bring into question the whole nature of the project. For many years the RCMP had been the most visible sign of government power; as well as upholding the law, they administered government relief and were responsible for handing out child allowances. You would have been a brave man to say no when a six-foot Mounty repeatedly turned up at your doorstep inviting you to take part in a plan which he was obviously so keen on.

Three sites were chosen for the experimental locations. Alexandra Fjord and Craig Harbour on Ellesmere Island were both thought to be rich in game and capable of sustaining a new community. No one had actually carried out a proper wildlife study in either area, but that was all part of the 'experiment'. Resolute Bay, slightly further south on Cornwallis Island, was different. It had been the site of a joint Canadian–American air force base since 1947 and was also home to a detachment of the Canadian Air Force. It was hoped that some of the Inuit would be able to find menial jobs at the base and another experiment could be staged to 'work out a method by which Eskimos may be trained to replace white employees in the North without Eskimo children losing touch with the native way of life'.

In March 1953 the deputy Minister for Northern Development rubber-stamped the project and four months later the *CD Howe* steamed into Port Harrison to pick up seven families comprising thirty-four people, including a pregnant woman and an eighty-year-old grandmother. During the voyage the natives and their thirty dogs were separated from the white crew and were fed only tea and hard tack biscuits for their lunch whilst the whites sat down to a full meal. John Amagoalik remembers how initial high spirits soon faded:

> *As a five-year-old the beginning of the journey was very*
> *exciting, it was a big adventure for myself and the other young*
> *people. But as the journey progressed and it took longer and*
> *longer and we kept going further and further and it became*
> *colder and colder, I remember starting to feel very*
> *uncomfortable.*

A month later the ship arrived at Pond Inlet in Baffin Island where three more Inuit families were picked up who had been chosen to teach the southerners how to hunt in the Arctic. That year ice conditions were so bad that the ship couldn't make it up to Alexandra Fjord so the group was split between Craig Harbour and Resolute. This was the first time the Inuit were told that the group was going to be split and many of them were deeply upset. The first batch were put ashore at Craig Harbour, though they were later moved to another site forty miles away at Grise Fjord. The remaining Inuit were decanted into a smaller boat and taken up to Resolute Bay. It was a scene which John Amagoliak would never forget.

It was like landing on the moon. Looked one way and looked the other and all we could see was gravel as far as the eye could see. There was absolutely nothing – no man-made objects, no houses, nothing. No vegetation, no animals, nothing.

Ironically, though perhaps not entirely co-incidentally, Resolute had been home to a Thule Eskimo village four hundred years before. The site had only recently been excavated by Canadian archaeologists and its presence fitted in nicely with the rather romantic notion that the experiment would also return the Inuit to their 'natural' state. The Thule people were the ancestors of the modern Inuit. They had abandoned Resolute when the Ice Age caused the area to become colder and all the caribou to migrate south. The Port Harrison Inuit had no such luck; they were there for the duration. In spite of trumpeting the relocation as an exciting government initiative, little had been done to make life easier for the new arrivals. Seven families had to share six tents. The department had authorised the RCMP to take out a loan to buy provisions for a trading post but they were far from generous. Supplies included five pounds of putty and 200 gallons of gasoline for a non-existent boat. The Inuit laughed at the 'snow knives' which were sent to help them to build igloos and found it very hard to find sufficient snow for their construction. Resolute had an average winter temperature sixteen degrees lower than at Port Harrison's but it had far less snow.

The Inuit were forced to scavenge wood from the base three miles away in order to build a hut which they could use as a community hall and for the trading post. Even before they left Quebec, the department officials had been informed by the Air Force that there were, in fact, no jobs for any Inuit on the base and that furthermore they had no intention of supporting the new arrivals if the experiment started to go badly. But the civil servants decided to go ahead anyway. A policy of strict segregation was enforced between the settlement and the base four miles away. This was motivated by genuine fears of the dangers of alcohol and of fraternisation between the white personnel and the Inuit women, but it was also part of the whole experimental project which was rapidly taking on the aspect of something between a survival test and a penal colony. Visitors to Resolute in the early fifties did note a far lower incidence of 'white man's' diseases amongst the Inuit which was in part due to this policy of segregation, but even if there were advantages the Inuit resented the restrictions which were placed on their freedom of movement. So great was Ottawa's fear of fraternisation that when in 1953 a CBC documentary showed the Inuit singing carols at the Air Force base and receiving Christmas presents, an enquiry was held and the RCMP officer Ross Gibson had to protest that he had bought all the presents out of his own pocket.

All the white officials in the project seemed to make the fundamental assumption that the Inuit would be happy wherever they were placed in the Arctic and that, in the great traditions of 'noble savagery', they would adapt quickly to the new conditions. In fact they found it very hard. In Port Harrison they never had to face the rigours of the Arctic winter and the dark period from late October to the middle of February. In Port Harrison there was a school and a nursing station; here there was a Mounty and a first aid kit. There the diet had been much more varied, including plenty of fish, birds and berries in the summer; here they had to exist primarily on sea mammals, though many of them were unfamiliar with the requisite hunting techniques. Although the project was supposed to be bringing them back to the land, the Inuit were severely restricted when it came to hunting caribou and musk oxen because the area had been designated a game reserve. In the first few years many of the Inuit remember going hungry and having to trawl the local garbage dump for food thrown out by the white personnel. John Amagoalik used to look forward to the arrival of incoming flights to the base because he knew that there would soon be rich pickings from unfinished airline food. The dump was supposed to be out of bounds, but Officer Gibson wryly commented in his report from 1954 that a lot of foxes were caught there.

After a couple of years the Inuit began to get used to the new hunting conditions and were able to begin to pay back the loan that the department had forced them to take out to set up the trading post. However, there were frequent disagreements between the RCMP on the ground and the officials back in Ottawa over the level of support given to the Inuit. The RCMP officers argued that the Inuit were having to pay an unfair mark-up on the price of goods bought at the store and were outraged that the department was actually making a substantial profit from the sale of the Inuit furs at auction. Because only a limited number of items were available at the government-run trading post, the RCMP were ordered to allow the Inuit to purchase 'only what they might reasonably require'. The Inuit were never paid in cash and they were given little information on the state of their accounts at the trading post until 1960, when it was transformed into a local Co-Op.

But the restriction which the Inuit resented most was that, in spite of the promises that they could return after two years, they were effectively prevented from going back to Port Harrison. Again the officials seemed to have fundamentally underestimated the Inuit attachment to their homeland. The Inuit were a nomadic race, but left to their own devices they generally limited their movements to a fairly small area, and migrations of this kind were virtually unheard of. In those days there were no telephones and mail deliveries were erratic at the best of times. The Inuit were quite simply lonely. 'It was mentioned every day,' remembers John Amagoalik, 'I think my mother cried almost every day because she was so homesick, because she missed her relatives and friends.' White workers at the weather station received free housing, free transport allowances and were paid special bonuses for their time in the north. The Inuit believed that they had been given a guarantee that they could return to Port Harrison after two years if they so desired, but they could not do so without the help of the government officials, who were far from accommodating. The supply ship in which they had arrived only visited Port Harrison on the outward leg of its journey, and the Inuit were told that if they wanted to return they would have to make their own travel arrangements. It was suggested to one Inuit who wrote to the department in 1961 that if he wanted to return he would have to purchase an aeroplane ticket from Kuujuak which would cost $2000, a totally unrealistic sum. The officials even discouraged movement between the two new settlements at Grise Fjord and Resolute; when three families from Grise Fjord asked to be relocated to Resolute they were firmly persuaded that this was not a good idea at all.

Initially the Department of Indian Affairs was very pleased with the project and in 1955 three more families were brought up to Resolute, but as the decade progressed official policies changed. In 1958 there was a disastrous relocation of the Ahiarmiut from Manitoba, a tribe Farley Mowat had written about six years earlier. Six people died and two were murdered. A new plan emerged to create larger settlements in the areas which the Inuit currently occupied. Instead of bringing them back to the land, the government decided that education was the key to development in the north. In 1955 there were 380 Inuit attending schools in the Northwest Territories; by 1963 that number had grown to 2494.

The late sixties and early seventies were a period of intense activity in the Arctic. After the 1968 Alaskan oil strike the petrol and mineral companies descended on the region determined to tap its potential. At one stage there were more than forty exploration firms working out of Resolute, making its airport one of the busiest in Canada. In 1969 the Queen visited Resolute leaving a trail of fond memories and autographed photographs behind her. One of the less impressive souvenirs of her visit was an official car park built on top of some of the most important Thule archaeological sites. Then came ambitious plans to turn Resolute into a model, racially integrated northern settlement. The renowned Anglo-Scandinavian architect Ralph Erskine was brought in to design a brand-new town which would be covered with a glass dome and have its own trees and a shopping mall. Erskine's scheme came to nothing, but today you can still see its legacy on the outskirts of town where a rather incongruous curved terrace languishes in disrepair.

For the Inuit this was a period of increased freedom and more opportunities of work at the base, but it was a mixed blessing. The Arctic Circle bar became infamous for its drunken Inuit, selling their wives for a round of drinks. The death of Joseph Idlout was a sad epitaph to the myth of the heroic Inuit. In the early fifties he had become famous in Canada as the proud hunter who was the star of Doug Wilkinson's influential documentary *Land of the Long Day*. He had appeared on the back of the two-dollar bill and had been awarded the Coronation Medal in 1953 . He was relocated from Pond Inlet to Resolute Bay in 1955 at his own request but he found it increasingly difficult to fit into the modern Arctic. In 1968 he died in a snow-mobiling accident after a night at the Arctic Circle bar.

As the decades progressed, however, the Inuit grew much stronger as a political force. The first Inuk was elected to the council of the Northwest Territories in 1966 and 1971 saw the formation of the Inuit Tapirisat of Canada (ITC) which would soon become a powerful lobby group fighting for native rights. In 1969 when the government published a white paper proposing that it should no longer legally recognise Indian reserves there was a huge wave of protest. When they negotiated a land claim agreement with the Indians and Inuit of northern Quebec in 1975 as part of their plan to build a huge hydroelectric power plant, they were forced to agree to a compensation package worth $225 million over ten years. The Inuit 'elders' of Grise Fjord and Resolute began to move back to Port Harrison in the mid-seventies initially at their own expense, but in 1982 the ITC and its new president John Amagoalik wrote to the Department of Indian Affairs and Northern Development demanding that the government should honour its earlier promise and pay for the return trips. When the government prevaricated, a campaign grew demanding compensation and ultimately an official apology from the government for its treatment of its 'human guinea-pigs' in the High Arctic. This reached a climax in 1993 when a series of hearings took place in the full glare of publicity in downtown Ottawa before the government's own Royal Commission for Aboriginal Peoples.

The case of the 'High Arctic Exiles' received massive public sympathy because of the immensely moving testimony of the Inuit witnesses. But on top of the human tragedy there was another element: the Inuit and their supporters alleged that not only did the government pressurise them into taking part in a highly dubious 'experiment' but that they did so under false pretences. They claimed that one of the main motives for the relocation was to bolster Canadian sovereignty in the Arctic in the face of US expansionism. Canada's relationship with its southern neighbour has always been a touchy issue, and throughout this century successive governments had continually worried about perceived threats to Canada's control over the Arctic. Were the Inuit, as they claimed, 'human flag-poles'? Sovereignty was a complex issue with a long and tangled history.

In 1880 Britain formally transferred ownership of its High Arctic territories to Canada, though at that time no one knew exactly how far they extended. Implicit in the hand-over was the idea of forestalling US expansionism in the area. In 1868 the USA had bought Alaska from Russia for $7.2 million and the US Secretary of State, William Henry Seward, had wanted to buy Greenland as well. Early US and Scandinavian explorers regarded most of the High Arctic as 'no man's land'. Amundsen dreamed of discovering new territory between the North Pole and Alaska and his fellow Norwegian Otto Sverdrup actually claimed the islands to the west of Ellesmere for Norway. In 1930 the Norwegians formally recognised Canadian sovereignty in the area but only after they received a payment of $67,000 to compensate for Sverdrup's work. In the 1920s Canada began a policy of sending out RCMP 'flag detachments' to some of the more remote islands in the hope that such a visible show of force would confirm their ownership of the area. They even introduced a bill in 1925 requiring all future explorers to get a licence before they entered what Canada deemed to be its territories.

American activity in the Arctic increased dramatically during the Second World War. A string of air-bases and weather stations were built across the Arctic known as the 'crimson corridor' in anticipation of ferrying wounded US soldiers back from Europe. The US also took over responsibility for the defence of Greenland, where they built two major airfields, and in the early fifties there were plans for more airstrips on uninhabited islands. In response the Canadian government attempted to pursue a policy of 'Canadianisation', insisting that there should be Canadian personnel present at Arctic military installations and, initially at least, that Canada should reimburse the United States for the cost of establishing the bases.

A recently released secret Cabinet document revealed that in the fifties the US presence in the Arctic was causing serious concern at the top levels of government. Dated 13 January 1953, it noted that there were as many permanent and more transient US citizens in the Arctic as Canadians and worried that if current plans for forty radar stations were realised, then the whole issue of Canadian sovereignty might be called into question: 'If Canadian claims to the territory in the Arctic rested on discovery and continuous occupation, Canadian claims to some relatively unexplored areas might be questioned in the future.' No one in the government thought that they were about to be invaded, but there were real fears, that with their huge defence commitment to the Arctic, the United States would effectively take over if Canada just sat back and did nothing. It wasn't simply a question of military strategy: from the fifties onwards the government was aware of the region's huge potential in terms of raw materials.

The influential Cantley report of 1950 looked into the changing importance of the Canadian Arctic:

> *Instead of a hinterland it has become a potential frontier and as such it quite evidently interests other countries than our own. It would appear that we will have to revise our attitude towards the Arctic and take a much greater interest in its affairs than we have done in the past.*

In order to cement their claims, the government recognised that it needed to maintain 'effective occupation' of the Arctic and there were some officials who believed that one of the best ways of doing this was by populating the region with Inuit. Ben Sivertz, one of the officials most closely associated with the programme, told the Canadian Air Force in August 1953, with reference to the relocation to Resolute, that: 'The Canadian government is anxious to have Canadians occupying as much of the Arctic as possible and it appeared that in many cases the Eskimo were the only people capable of doing this.'

The idea that there might have been another agenda behind the 'experiment' made absolute sense to relocated Inuit like John Amagoalik and George Echalook. They had never quite understood why the government had sent them off to such a remote location until they started researching into government files:

> *They were using us. They wanted the Queen Elizabeth Islands to be part of Canada. It was a really big thing for them. They thought the islands were really rich. Later on we found out what a big thing it was for them. But not for us . . . We have mixed feelings about this – on the one hand we feel bad because we weren't told that they were doing this for sovereignty reasons, but at the same time we feel good because we did contribute to Canadian sovereignty. We might have agreed if they had just been honest with us. But they didn't. Instead they lied and gave us false information and didn't tell us the whole story.*

The Canadian press instantly latched on to the idea that sovereignty might have been part of the story and that the fate of the High Arctic

Exiles might have been tied up with Cold War politics. At the Royal Commission hearings in 1993 the former officials who had organised the relocation vigorously denied everything; they insisted that sovereignty was never part of the equation and maintained that the relocation was for the Inuit's own good. In the words of one journalist, the officials came 'with their walking sticks, their hearing aids and their indignation' and they were willing to fight back. Graham Rowley, for many years one of the government's most trusted advisers on northern matters, claimed that the Inuit were exaggerating their hardship in order to gain compensation: 'The Inuit have now been indoctrinated to think of themselves as victims, however much of this runs against the evidence and the written testimony of their elders.' Gordon Robertson, for most of the sixties Canada's senior civil servant, was adamant that history was being rewritten at the expense of the dedicated officials who conceived of the relocation:

> I think it is quite a travesty of justice to have their motives
> misinterpreted, to have them held up to ridicule because they
> did something honestly, earnestly and selflessly, on the best of
> motives and with the interest of the Inuit people only in mind.

The two groups – the white officials and the Inuit relocatees – gave their testimony in two different sessions in two different buildings and to many people it still seemed as if they were still living in two different worlds. Even if many of the officials were genuinely concerned with the welfare of the Inuit, there is no doubt that many of the Inuit did feel homesick and were for many years frustrated in their wish to return to Quebec. In 1988, when the government agreed to pay for relocation costs, nineteen of the original relocatees left Grise Fjord and at one stage the settlement was so depleted it was almost closed down. All but three of the original settlers left Resolute, though most of their children, who had been born there and now had families of their own, decided to stay.

In 1994 the Royal Commission published a highly critical report which stated that the relocations had been fundamentally flawed, that sovereignty considerations had indeed played an important role in the project and that the government should now both apologise to the Inuit and offer a compensation package. In March 1996 an agreement was finally drawn up between the Department of Indian Affairs and Northern

Development and the representatives of the Inuit which acknowledged that the 'High Arctic Exiles encountered hardship, suffering and loss both individually and collectively' and agreed to set up a trust fund for the Inuit and their relatives totalling $10 million. However, they refused to give any apology and furthermore they only agreed to pay compensation if the Inuit signed a document stating that: 'The High Arctic Relocatees hereby recognise and acknowledge that in planning the relocation to the High Arctic the government officials of the time were acting with honourable intentions in what was perceived to be in the best interests of the Inuit.' For the Inuit this was a bitter pill, but they had grown weary of continually pressing their claim and now wanted to move on and put the events behind them. Though the ink has now dried, the arguments still rage on and both camps remain bitter.

Resolute still suffers from many of the problems encountered by the original relocatees. There are now regular scheduled flights in and out of town but it is still a remote and unforgiving place to live. In the seventies the village gained a reputation for alcoholism and drug abuse but today it is a much happier community. Most of the current Inuit residents were either born in Resolute or came there by their own choice. The mayor, George Echalook, is now more concerned with getting better facilities for the residents than with the geo-political considerations of sovereignty. Resolute has a slightly unreal quality though: nearly all of the whites still live at the air-base, and the one hotel in the village, the High Arctic Lodge, has somewhat the air of an international zone. Outside there is a signpost with arrows pointing to London, New York and the North Pole. Every year people come here from all over the world to organise their various expeditions to the Arctic. The locals rarely mix with the intrepid explorers whom they have wryly dubbed the 'ice-mice'. Down the road, the Canadian Polar Shelf project increasingly plays host to teams of scientists who use Resolute as a base for their high-tech scientific projects. The airport is relatively quiet now. Planes still fly out to service the giant Polaris mine on Little Cornwallis Island, but for the moment the glory days of the oil prospectors are over. It no longer hangs at the airport, but the sign which used to greet visitors still rings true:

Welcome to Resolute, pronounced Desolate, nothing around for miles and miles but miles and miles.

POSTSCRIPT

We arrived in the Arctic and a couple of hours later we were out on the ice filming the Women's Polar Relay team. The first all-female expedition, they were sponsored by Penguin McVitie to the tune of 7000 chocolate bars and an undisclosed sum in cash. On 27 May they finally made it to the Pole in spite of terrible weather and atrocious ice conditions. In 1997 we counted fifteen different expeditions to the North Pole. Some went from Siberia, some went from Canada, the polar veteran Will Steger took a Russian ice-breaker to the Pole and tried to work his way back to land. The lure of the Arctic is as strong as ever, but the modern Arctic traveller is a very different creature from Peary and Franklin.

Today's Icemen – and women – are adventurers rather than explorers. They may still crave fame, but it is their feats of stamina which win applause rather than the news they bring back of lands unknown. 'Unsupported' is the new buzzword for the polar wannabe: to go from land to the North Pole without being re-supplied by air. When Peary set off for the Pole he had no choice but to be unsupported: emergency satellite beacons hadn't been invented and the Wright brothers had only flown the Kittyhawk off the drawing board six years previously. Today's adventurers deliberately do it the hard way. More than ever before, the Arctic is a place to make inner journeys, to test yourself against the elements and your own weaknesses. The Japanese explorer Mitsuro Obah gets 1997's prize for dedication after succeeding on his fourth attempt to walk across the Arctic Ocean from Russia to Canada via the North Pole. In 1995 he lost all of his toes and several fingers. This time frostbite reeked havoc with his upper lip and his nose but he made it in the end.

Three expeditions failed to reach their goal, including the first joint Anglo-Norwegian expedition which was supposed to put an end to the age-old rivalry between the sons of Scott and Amundsen. David Hempleman Adams and Rune Gjedness's attempt will, however, be remembered for its extraordinary rescue of Alan Bywater, a 21-one-year-old British student, who had been attempting a solo journey to the Pole. Ten days from land he fell through the ice, losing his emergency beacon and only narrowly avoiding losing his life. With incredible good fortune, he managed to pick up the tracks of the Anglo-Norwegian expedition and to their utter amazement he staggered into their camp where he waited for a rescue plane. Hempleman Adams and Gjedness carried on but, with one of their sledges badly damaged, they were forced to stop.

The last great pioneering Arctic journey was made by a British team lead by Wally Herbert. In 1968 they set off to cross the Arctic Ocean from Point Barrow in Alaska to Spitsbergen using dog teams, true grit and the polar drift for propulsion. On 6 April 1969 they became the first British team to reach the North Pole but it took them almost fifteen months to complete their 3500-mile journey. Almost twenty years later Herbert became embroiled in the Peary/Cook controversy when he was invited by the *National Geographic* to write a preface for Peary's soon-to-be-published expedition diary. This had lain hidden in a family vault for many years and hadn't even been surrendered to the Naval commit-tee which examined Peary's case in 1911. The *National Geographic* chose Herbert because he was such a respected explorer, but when his research cast further doubt on Peary's claim they decided not to publish the diary and a couple of years later commissioned the self-styled 'Navigation Foundation' to have yet another look at the issue. It came to quite different conclusions from Wally Herbert and once more endorsed Peary's claim, which had been backed for so many years by the *National Geographic*. The diary itself is now available for anyone to see at the US National Archives in Washington. It is most notable for what it leaves out rather than what it includes: between April 6 and 8, the days when Peary claimed to be at the Pole, there are no entries at all save a loose-leaf page which was inserted from another notebook con-taining the famous 'goal of centuries' quotation.

The controversy still rages on and even in 1997 there were two new books which promised to hand out the prize once and for all. Robert Bryce's epic study *Cook and Peary: The Polar Controversy Resolved* concluded that neither man actually reached the Pole. In spite of its 1120 pages, the Frederick Cook Society has vowed that this is not the last word on the subject. In his book *Robert Peary and Matthew Henson at the North Pole*, William Mollet, a retired Air Force navigator, claims to have come up with a plausible theory of how Peary could have navigated without taking longitude sightings. Long-time aficionados of the controversy and old Arctic hands remain sceptical.

The title of Mollet's book reflects the growing stature of Matthew Henson, Peary's black assistant. When they came back from the Arctic, the *National Geographic* awarded the *Roosevelt*'s captain, Bob Bartlett, a medal but didn't consider Henson to be worthy of such an honour. Today Bartlett is pretty much forgotten but Henson has been elevated to the status of the first black explorer, graced a US postage stamp, and had a naval ship named after him. In 1988, with the full support of Ronald Reagan, he was re-interred in Arlington cemetery just yards from Peary's monument. Peary was always ambiguous about Henson and there are no records of any personal contact between the two men after 1910, but ironically Henson's ascending Pole Star is now shining down on his erstwhile master.

Whilst die-hards on both sides continue to fight their man's corner, and as more people have actually made surface journeys to the Pole, so scepticism has grown about both claims. If there is any sort of consensus, Peary's claim is taken far more seriously than Cook's, but though many accept that he may have got pretty close, few believe that he actually made it. It is doubtful that the controversy will ever be resolved: in the end it all depends on faith rather than evidence and no one can categorically deny that either man was telling the truth.

In 1969 the Northwest Passage was once more in the headlines when an American oil tanker, the *SS Manhattan* made the first successful commercial voyage from Alaska to the east coast of the USA. In the following year they made another attempt but this time they failed. The ice conditions are just too unpredictable for any regular traffic. The US ice-breaker *Polar Sea* repeated the journey in 1984 without seeking permission from Canada which was quick to condemn this violation of its sovereignty.

All of the Arctic states are now keenly encouraging tourism in the region, though it remains to be seen whether this will ever really take off. Few but the most well booted of Arctic buffs can afford the $5000 champagne flight to the Pole or the more leisurely trip by Russian ice-breaker which comes in at a cool $18,300 per head. That said, legend has it in Resolute that one Japanese businessman splashed out on his very own plane to transport himself and his lover to the Pole for some high-latitude ecstasy.

With the end of the Cold War, the Arctic states now have a new agenda for the region. Though no shots were ever actually fired – or so we are told officially – the militarisation of the region has not gone without its 'collateral' damage. Between 1955 and 1990, the Soviet Union used the Arctic as one of its main nuclear testing grounds, exploding forty-two underground bombs and staging ninety-two atmospheric explosions on the Novaya Zemlya islands in the eastern Arctic. Until comparatively recently, the Soviets used the Arctic as nuclear waste dump, despatching no less than sixteen reactors to a watery grave. Though they are now finally beginning to face up to their responsibilities, there are very real fears that the residual radiation will cause long-term damage to the region and Russian scientists have already recorded a marked deterioration in the health of people living around Archangel, one of the principal Arctic ports. On the American side, workers employed to dismantle the DEW Line stations in northern Canada have found dangerous concentrations of highly toxic substances around the sites. Many of the old cold warriors have now turned into environmental peace-niks but it seems unlikely that either the American or the Russian governments will be willing to put so much money into polar science now that there is no military justification.

The Arctic's climate makes it particularly vulnerable to environmental damage. Pollutants which might be dispersed quickly in other parts of the world persist for decades. The reliance of native peoples on fresh, locally hunted meat increases the immediate human impact of this kind of damage. In 1994 concentrations of dangerous chemicals found in the breast milk of Inuit women were seven times higher than in women from southern Ontario. In recent years much attention has focused on the dangers of ozone depletion over the polar regions causing an increase in UV-B radiation which can inflict long-term damage on both humans and animals. More immediately worrying are the menacingly titled 'trans-border pollutants', dangerous industrial by-products from as far away as south-east Asia which migrate northwards.

The last two decades have seen renewed emphasis on Inuit rights all across the Arctic. Though Greenland remains tied to Denmark, for many years its population has enjoyed a considerable say in the country's future. In 1985 they made an unprecedented decision to leave the EEC, although their economy is still very closely linked to Europe's. During the Soviet years the Inuit tribes of the Russian Arctic were subject to the same collectivisation policies that were active in the rest of the country, though the government did try to protect many of the unique aspects of their culture. Today there is much less intervention but they have been left with the mess created by unfettered oil and mineral exploration in the region. Though there are few official figures available, it seems that the population of the Russian Arctic has declined significantly in recent years after the government stopped subsidising Russians who chose to emigrate to the northern frontiers.

The Canadian Arctic has gone through a period of considerable change over the last two decades. The Inuit now have two television channels, they own the main airline, and in 1993 Prime Minister Brian Mulroney signed a historic treaty agreeing to pay $1.17 billion in compensation over the next fourteen years and to create a new northern territory, Nunavut, in which for the foreseeable future they will have a guaranteed majority. It covers one-fifth of the whole of Canada, though it only contains 22,000 people. The first elections are due to take place in 1999 and ten years later it will become a fully fledged province. The Inuit politicians overseeing the transition have ambitious plans to combine the best of traditional values with a truly modern approach to everything from nature conservation to female political representation.

Since the first major oil strike in 1969 at Prudhoe Bay, it has been clear that the Arctic has huge raw material resources. However, it is still prohibitively expensive to exploit this wealth and though governments may now respect the Inuit right to enjoy the fruits of future development, there is no guarantee that this will ever generate any significant amounts of money. Undoubtedly the creation of Nunavut is a major step forward, but many Arctic settlements still feel that they are caught between two worlds. The elders often still live off locally hunted 'country food' but many of the younger people are more familiar with chocolate-coated 'Eskimo pies' from the local supermarket than with the techniques of building an igloo or living off the land. In Hall Beach or Resolute you see large hunks of meat freezing outside people's houses, destined to be fed to the teams of sled-dogs who are chained to jerrycans on the outskirts of town. But you also see heaps of abandoned cars rusting in the snow and young men tearing along the high street on souped-up snowmobiles, all wrapped up and no place to go. When we were talking to one of the original settlers relocated from northern Quebec the local mayor had to interrupt the interview to deliver the sad news that two young men had just committed suicide at another settlement. One was a relative, the other a friend.

On today's map many Arctic place names have changed, the references to past explorers replaced by traditional Inuit words. Frobisher Bay has become Iqaluit, Port Harrison has become Innukjuak, Resolute has become Qausuittuq. Long before any of the European and American explorers turned up to conquer the Arctic, the Inuit had learnt how to live with it. When Peary returned to his base in Greenland in 1909 claiming to have 'nailed the stars and stripes to the Pole' he hoped that such an achievement would bring him fame all around the world. The four Eskimos who accompanied him were greeted warmly by their friends and relatives, having been away for so many months, but they were not treated as heroes. If they had returned with seal or walrus meat for the community then they would have been great men, but to have come back with a symbolic victory meant little. In a land where the climate is so dominant, the Inuit have an appropriate metaphor for the white men: 'They are like the weather: they come for a couple of years and you enjoy them being there but you know that they will not stay, and soon they will be gone.'

BIBLIOGRAPHY

Chapter One:

Pierre Berton: *The Arctic Grail* (Viking/New York, 1988). Chauncey Loomis: *Weird and Tragic Shores* (University of Nebraska Press/Lincoln,1991). Frances Woodward: *Portrait of Jane: A Life of Lady Franklin* (Hodder and Stoughton/London, 1951). Kenneth J Carpenter: *A History of Scurvy and Vitamin C* (Cambridge University Press/Cambridge, 1987). Augustine Courtauld (ed.): *From the Ends of the Earth – an Anthology of Polar Writing* (Oxford University Press/London, 1958). Leopold McClintock: *A Narrative of the Discovery of the Fate of Sir John Franklin and his Companions* (Ticknor and Fields/Boston, 1860). Charles Dickens: *The Lost Arctic Voyagers* (in *Household Words*, issues 245, 246, 248, 249, 1854). John Brown: *Arctic Scrapbook* (Scott Polar Research Institute/Unpublished).

Chapters Two and Three:

Robert E Peary: *The North Pole* (Hodder and Stoughton/London, 1910); *Nearest the Pole* (Hutchinson/London, 1907); *Northward Over the Great Ice* (Methuen/London, 1898). Wally Herbert: *The Noose of Laurels* (Hodder and Stoughton/London, 1989). John Edward Weems: *Peary – the Explorer and the Man* (Eyre and Spottiswoode/London, 1967). Dr Frederick Cook: *Through the First Antarctic Night* (Heinemann/London, 1900); *My Attainment of the Pole* (The Polar Publishing Company/New York, 1911); *Return from the Pole* (Pellegrini and Cudahy/New York, 1951). Matthew Henson: *A Black Explorer at the North Pole* (University of Nebraska Press/London, 1989). Robert M Bryce: *Cook & Peary, the Polar Controversy Resolved* (Stackpole Books/Pennsylvania, 1997). Bradley Robinson: *Dark Companion* (Hodder and Stoughton/London, 1948). William Mollet: *Robert Peary and Matthew Henson at the North Pole* (Elkhorn Press/Kentucky, 1996).

Chapter Four:
Dr Salomon Andrée, Nils Strindberg, and Knut Fraenkel: *The Andrée Diaries* (Bodley Head/London, 1931). Vilhjalmur Stefansson: *Unsolved Mysteries of the Arctic* (Macmillan/New York, 1945). Gosta H Liljequist: *High Latitudes: a History of Swedish Polar Travels and Research* (Swedish Polar Research Secretariat/Stockholm). Per Olof Sundman: *The Flight of the Eagle* (Pantheon Books/New York, 1970).

Chapter Five:
Roald Amundsen: *My Life as an Explorer* (Heinemann/London, 1927); *My Polar Flight* (Hutchinson/London, 1925); *First Crossing of the Polar Sea* (with Lincoln Ellsworth. Doubleday/New York, 1928). Lincoln Ellsworth: *Beyond Horizons* (Book League of America/New York, 1938). Umberto Nobile: *My Polar Flights* (Muller/London, 1961); *Navigating the 'Norge' from Rome to the North Pole and Beyond* (National Geographic Magazine, July 1927). John Grierson: *Challenge to the Poles* (Foulis/London, 1964).

Chapter Six:
Umberto Nobile: *With the Italia to the North Pole* (Allen and Unwin/London, 1930). Odd Arnesen: *The Polar Adventure: the 'Italia' Tragedy Seen at Close Quarters* (Victor Gollancz/London, 1929). Einar Lundborg: *The Arctic Rescue – how Nobile was Saved* (Viking Press/New York, 1929). Rolf S Tandberg: *The 'Italia' Disaster: Fact and Fantasy* (published by the author/Oslo, 1977). Wilbur Cross: *Ghost Ship of the Pole* (Heinemann/London).

Chapter Seven:
F Spencer Chapman: *Northern Lights* (Chatto and Windus/London, 1933). J M Scott: *Gino Watkins* (Hodder and Stoughton/London, 1935); *The Private Life of Polar Exploration* (Blackwood/Edinburgh, 1982). Martin Lindsay: *Those Greenland Days* (Blackwood/Edinburgh, 1932). Augustine Courtauld: *Man the Ropes* (Hodder and Stoughton/London, 1957). Nicholas Wollaston: *The Man on the Ice Cap* (Constable/London, 1980). Andrew Croft: *Polar Exploration* (Black/London, 1947).

Chapter Eight:
Sir Alexander Glen: *Footholds Against a Whirlwind* (Hutchinson/

London, 1975). Douglas Liversidge: *The Third Front,* (Severn House Publishers, 1976). Ernest Schofield and Roy Conyers Nesbit: *Arctic Airmen,* (Kimber/London, 1987). Bernt Balchen: *War Below Zero* (Allen and Unwin/London, 1945). Thor B. Arlov: *A Short History of Svalbard* (Norsk Polarinstitutt/Oslo, 1994). William Barr: *Wettertrupp Haudegan* in Polar Record 23-143 (Scott Polar Research Institute/Cambridge, 1986). Olav Farnes: *The War in the Arctic* (Darf/London, 1991).

Chapter Nine:
Sir Hubert Wilkins: *Under the North Pole* (Brewer, Warren and Putnam/ New York, 1931). James Calvert: *Surface at the Pole* (Hutchinson/ London, 1961). John Grierson: *Challenge to the Poles* (Foulis/London, 1964) Paul Lashmar: *Spy Flights of the Cold War* (Sutton/Stroud, 1996). Charles Daugherty: *City Under the Ice* (MacMillan/New York, 1963). Eva Freeman: *MIT Lincoln Laboratory: Technology in the National Interest* (published by MIT/Massachusetts, 1995). Bernt Balchen: *Come North With Me* (Hodder and Stoughton/London, 1959). MIT Lincoln Laboratory: *Report of Summer Study Group* (unpublished/Massachusetts, 1952).

Chapter Ten:
Alan Rudolph Marcus: *Relocating Eden* (University Press of New England/Hanover, 1995). Farley Mowat: *The People of the Deer* (Souvenir Press/London, 1989). Kevin McMahon: *Arctic Twilight* (Lorimer and Company, 1988). *The High Arctic Relocation* (Royal Commission on Aboriginal Peoples/Ottawa, 1994). Shelagh Grant: *A Case of Compounded Error* (published in *Northern Perspectives* magazine/Ottawa, 1991).

INDEX